DON'T PANIC

YOU MUST READ THE FOLLOWING BEFORE CONTINUING

In the first decades of the 21st century, the volume of the radio and television transmissions we send out into the universe has expanded exponentially. You can add to this the various objects we've fired into space over the years, including NASA's Voyager probe, which was launched almost 40 years ago and has just entered interstellar space, heading for the mysterious Oort cloud. But can we be sure whoever is out there is friendly?

These activities of ours are like sending an open invitation to every other life form in the blackness of space. And the invitation reads, 'Please come and take my planet!' Not surprisingly, we have already attracted interest from aliens and we know of at least four extra-terrestrial species who are either intervening in human affairs or preparing invasion plans against us. The alien threat to Earth is no longer science fiction – it's science fact!

This manual is designed to provide you with the latest scientific insight and intelligence on aliens and their plans to take over our planet. This information will ensure that you're equipped not only to resist abductions, invasive implants and survive an alien invasion, but also to lead a human fight-back and even take the war to the alien home world.

Published by the Ministry of Alien Defence in London, this volume calls on a vast wealth of knowledge and experience, from access to secret US Air Force UFO files and abduction case studies to evidence from the latest alien vehicle crash site in China and top-secret plans for the creation of a united Earth defence force. The United Nations Office for Earth Defence has been heavily involved in ensuring that the facts and figures within this volume are the best we have. Even if you count yourself as a sceptic, please do read on as we present here, for the first time, all information on the known species that may soon invade our planet.

This manual is not designed for astronauts, boffins or eggheads. It's for everyone. In true Haynes style, we aim to demonstrate how with the right knowledge, training and the largest available roll of aluminium foil, the concerned citizen can really hit ET where it hurts. You can protect your home and family from mind-bending abductions, you can ensure that you remain free of any sinister implants, and you can determine which shape-shifting lizards are working to take over society.

But for now, put on your tin-foil hat and read on. A strange and sometimes frightening world is about to open up for you.

Sean T. Page
Ministry of Alien Defence, London

CONTENTS

ALIENS – FACT OR FICTION?   6

THE ALIEN FOOTPRINT ON EARTH   8
GREAT ALIEN MYTHS   10
THE UK PERSPECTIVE   12

ALIEN KNOWLEDGE 101   14

ALIENS IN JUDGEMENT   16
THE GREYS (ROSWELL GREYS, ZETANS)   18
LITTLE GREEN MEN (LGM, MARTIANS)   22
DRACONIANS (THE FIRST ONES, REPTILIANS)   26
INSECTOIDS (THE HIVE, THE SPECIES)   30
NORDIC (MIRROR MAN, GLIMMER MAN)   36

A HISTORY OF ALIEN CONTACT   40

PRE-HISTORY (UP TO 1939)   42
THE MODERN ERA (1939–80)   44
AREA 51 (DREAMLAND)   46
THE BATTLE OF DULCE AIRBASE   48
THE POST–ROSWELL ERA (1980 ONWARDS)   50

ALIEN CONTACT AND ABDUCTION   52

FIRST-CONTACT PROTOCOLS   54
ALIENS AND THE LAW   56
ALIEN ABDUCTIONS   58
EYE-WITNESS ACCOUNTS   60
ALIEN IMPLANTS   62
CATTLE MUTILATION   64

BECOMING AN ET PREPPER — 66

GETTING THE LOOK — 68
HOME-MADE PROTECTION — 70
PREPPING FOR FAMILIES — 72
ET PREPPER PRODUCTS — 74
HOME DEFENCE — 76
ABDUCTION PROOFING THE HOME — 78
THE PERFECT ALIEN INVASION BUNKER — 80

ALIEN COMBAT — 82

COMBAT AGAINST GREYS — 84
COMBAT AGAINST LITTLE GREEN MEN — 86
COMBAT AGAINST DRACONIANS — 88
COMBAT AGAINST INSECTOIDS — 90
ESCAPING FROM A HOLDING CELL — 92
ESCAPE SCENARIOS — 94

GUIDELINES FOR MILITARY FORCES — 96

ALIEN VIEWS OF HUMANITY — 98
FULL-SCALE PLANETARY ASSAULT — 100
STOPPING THE GREYS — 102
LIMITED-SCALE PLANETARY ASSAULT — 104
STOPPING THE LITTLE GREEN MEN — 106
A COVERT TAKEOVER — 108
STOPPING THE DRACONIANS — 110
AN ALIEN WAR OF EXTERMINATION — 112
STOPPING THE INSECTOIDS — 114

DEFENDING OUR PLANET — 116

DEFENCE IN SPACE — 118

ALIEN INVASION EXAMS — 122

ALIENS – FACT OR FICTION?

This volume is about the interference of alien life in human affairs. This could be friendly – we certainly hope so. But most experts agree that an alien presence is more likely to be hostile, ranging from spying and abductions to a full-scale invasion of Earth.

Before even planning for an alien invasion, it's important that you are up to date with all the facts. Perhaps you don't believe in life on other worlds, or that aliens would be interested in taking over our planet? Perhaps you think all these UFO and abduction stories are hoaxes? Well, read on. In this section we'll survey the published evidence to date and not only prove that aliens exist but that governments know about their existence.

? ARE WE ALONE?

Keep watching the skies!

The short answer is 'no'. This is the one area on which virtually every scientist agrees. Where do we start?

▶ We exist in a dodecahedron-shaped universe that's at least 150 billion light years wide – that's big. But to show how little we know about it, around 75% of the energy in the universe is made up of so-called 'dark energy' and we don't have much of a clue what that is.

▶ The universe is populated by billions of galaxies, some spiral-shaped, some elliptical and some in the shapes of amusing vegetables. Basically, there are loads of them!

▶ Since 2008 scientists working at United Nations Office for Earth Defence observatories have confirmed the existence of hundreds of Earth-like planets – and these are just the ones we can see. More theoretical studies have estimated that there are around 12,000 alien civilisations in our galaxy alone.

▶ As you'll discover as you read through this book, the final proof that we're not alone is the sheer number of alien sightings, abductions, implants and fiendish invasion plans being noted across the world every day – as well as the several ships, bodies and live extra-terrestrials that have been seized by Earth's various security agencies.

▶ To date, the world has comprehensive data on five known alien species in the universe, with fragmentary evidence suggesting the existence of over a hundred more. Out of these five, four appear to have hostile intentions towards humanity and our planet.

ALIENS – FACT OR FICTION?
DO YOU BELIEVE?

In a recent survey by the International Space Agency, over 50% of people reported that they had either experienced an alien encounter or firmly believed in their existence.

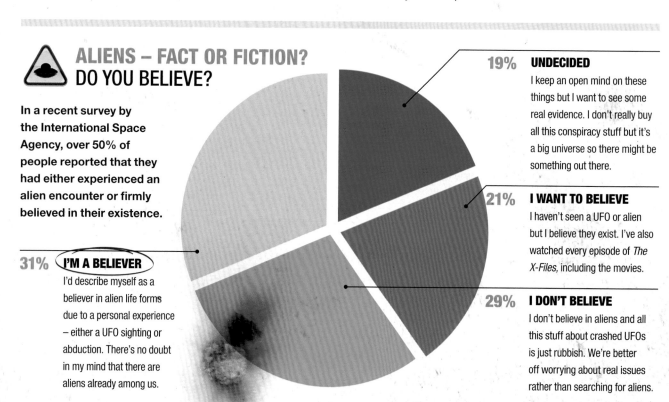

31% I'M A BELIEVER
I'd describe myself as a believer in alien life forms due to a personal experience – either a UFO sighting or abduction. There's no doubt in my mind that there are aliens already among us.

19% UNDECIDED
I keep an open mind on these things but I want to see some real evidence. I don't really buy all this conspiracy stuff but it's a big universe so there might be something out there.

21% I WANT TO BELIEVE
I haven't seen a UFO or alien but I believe they exist. I've also watched every episode of *The X-Files*, including the movies.

29% I DON'T BELIEVE
I don't believe in aliens and all this stuff about crashed UFOs is just rubbish. We're better off worrying about real issues rather than searching for aliens.

SURVEY OF 1,598 PEOPLE, MARCH 2014

DO YOU BELIEVE IN ALIENS?

Popular perception can only ever tell half of the story. Here at the Ministry of Alien Defence our stock-in-trade is hard facts. We have literally hundreds of case files, eye-witness accounts and alien artefacts that prove beyond all doubt not only that aliens exist in the universe but that they have also visited Earth many times. And, before you get a picture of us believers as a sectarian lunatic fringe, here's a list of famous people in history and what they have personally experienced or stated about extra-terrestrials. Browse through these quotes from military leaders, politicians and even former presidents. Remember, if you already believe, you're clearly not alone!

'I CAN ASSURE YOU THAT FLYING SAUCERS, GIVEN THAT THEY EXIST, ARE NOT CONSTRUCTED BY ANY POWER ON EARTH.'

PRESIDENT HARRY S. TRUMAN
33RD PRESIDENT OF THE UNITED STATES, 1950

'IF I BECOME PRESIDENT, I'LL MAKE EVERY PIECE OF INFORMATION THIS COUNTRY HAS ABOUT UFO SIGHTINGS AVAILABLE TO THE PUBLIC AND SCIENTISTS. I AM CONVINCED THAT UFOs EXIST BECAUSE I HAVE SEEN ONE.'

PRESIDENT JIMMY CARTER
DURING HIS PRESIDENTIAL CAMPAIGN, 1969

'THE PEOPLE'S REPUBLIC OF CHINA IS FULLY AWARE OF THE RISKS POSED BY THE ALIEN THREAT AND HAVE ACTED TO COUNTER THESE THREATS BOTH ON EARTH AND IN SPACE.'

GENERAL WANG LI-CHA
MILITARY LIAISON TO UNITED NATIONS IN NEW YORK, 2009

'I BELIEVE THAT THESE EXTRA-TERRESTRIAL VEHICLES AND THEIR CREWS ARE VISITING THIS PLANET FROM OTHER PLANETS... MOST ASTRONAUTS WERE RELUCTANT TO DISCUSS UFOs. I DID HAVE OCCASION IN 1951 TO HAVE TWO DAYS OF OBSERVATION OF MANY FLIGHTS OF THEM, OF DIFFERENT SIZES, FLYING IN FIGHTER FORMATION, GENERALLY FROM EAST TO WEST OVER EUROPE.'

MAJOR GORDON COOPER
NASA ASTRONAUT TO THE UNITED NATIONS, 1978

'THE UNITED STATES MILITARY ARE PREPARING WEAPONS THAT COULD BE USED AGAINST THE ALIENS, AND THEY COULD GET US INTO AN INTER-GALACTIC WAR WITHOUT US EVER HAVING ANY WARNING... THE BUSH ADMINISTRATION HAS FINALLY AGREED TO LET THE MILITARY BUILD A FORWARD BASE ON THE MOON, WHICH WILL PUT THEM IN A BETTER POSITION TO KEEP TRACK OF THE GOINGS AND COMINGS OF THE VISITORS FROM SPACE, AND TO SHOOT AT THEM, IF THEY SO DECIDE.'

PAUL THEODORE HELLYER
FORMER SENIOR MINISTER, CANADIAN PARLIAMENT, 2005

'THE NEXT WAR WILL BE AN INTER-PLANETARY WAR. THE NATIONS MUST SOME DAY MAKE A COMMON FRONT AGAINST ATTACK BY PEOPLE FROM OTHER PLANETS.'

DOUGLAS MACARTHUR
FORMER FIVE-STAR GENERAL OF THE US ARMY, 1955

'THE NUMBER OF PLANETS IN OUR GALAXY ON WHICH A TECHNOLOGICAL CIVILISATION IS NOW IN BEING IS ROUGHLY 530,000.'

ISAAC ASIMOV
EXTRA-TERRESTRIAL CIVILISATIONS, 1980

Pat down the chip shop said the same thing

'I'VE BEEN CONVINCED FOR A LONG TIME THAT THE FLYING SAUCERS ARE INTER-PLANETARY. WE ARE BEING WATCHED BY BEINGS FROM OUTER SPACE.'

ALBERT M. CHOP
DEPUTY PUBLIC RELATIONS DIRECTOR, NASA, 1965

'OF COURSE THE FLYING SAUCERS ARE REAL, AND THEY ARE INTER-PLANETARY.'

AIR CHIEF MARSHAL LORD DOWDING
CHIEF OF THE ROYAL AIR FORCE DURING WORLD WAR II, 1954

'WITH OUR OBSESSION WITH ANTAGONISMS OF THE MOMENT, WE OFTEN FORGET HOW MUCH UNITES ALL THE MEMBERS OF HUMANITY. I OCCASIONALLY THINK HOW QUICKLY OUR DIFFERENCES, WORLDWIDE, WOULD VANISH IF WE WERE FACING AN ALIEN THREAT FROM OUTSIDE THIS WORLD.'

PRESIDENT RONALD REAGAN
40TH PRESIDENT OF THE UNITED STATES, 1988

ALIENS – FACT OR FICTION?

THE ALIEN FOOTPRINT ON EARTH

Even if you're prepared to believe the vast weight of scientific evidence about life in other parts of the universe, you may still be sceptical as to whether aliens would ever make it to our isolated part of our very nondescript spiral galaxy. We'll take an in-depth look at alien motivation shortly, but for the moment consider these facts about UFO sightings and alien abductions.

UFO SIGHTINGS

Before the creation of the Ministry of Alien Defence in 1981, UFO sightings were collected by the RAF but other government agencies such as the Department for War and the National Health Service also gathered data separately, making it very difficult to consolidate an overall picture of sightings in the UK.

Since the creation of the Ministry hotline in 1989, things have thankfully become much clearer and we can now confirm some statistics concerning the number of people in the UK and Ireland who have reported UFO sightings.

Of course, these figures need to be read carefully. For example, these are 'verified reports', which means that they've been investigated by the 'Men in Black' and deemed 'viable sightings'. Investigating agencies tend to dismiss fanciful accounts or those from unreliable sources. However, it's important to consider that many of these may be sightings of the same alien ship. For instance, in 2009 a grey saucer entered UK airspace and flew the length of the country. Not surprisingly, the Ministry was bombarded with accounts of the vessel, with witnesses corroborating each other's stories with sketches of the ship and comments regarding its slow speed.

Our statistics confirm that the level of alien activity over the UK has certainly increased. Even if we allow for some inaccuracy in reporting, many other countries are experiencing the same trend. Basically, there are more and more alien craft visiting our planet and this is further supported by a disturbing growth in the number of abductions.

ALIENS – FACT OR FICTION?
RECORDED UFO SIGHTINGS

The following statistics are the UK's official figures on UFO sightings and include reports made by the RAF and other armed forces as well as members of the public.

Year	Sightings
1990	10,233
1995	12,666
2000	13,599
2005	16,322
2010	18,000
2015 estimate	22,000 +

> " IN MILITARY TERMS, IT WOULD SEEM THAT WE ARE BEING ASSESSED AND STUDIED. OUR ANALYSIS HAS SHOWN AN UNCOMFORTABLE CORRELATION BETWEEN UFO SIGHTINGS AND KEY MILITARY AND INFRASTRUCTURE INSTALLATIONS. LOOKING AT IT FROM A COLD AND STRATEGIC VIEWPOINT, OUR CAPABILITIES ARE BEING EXAMINED AND CATALOGUED BY FORCES FROM BEYOND OUR SPACE. "
> **GENERAL WILHELM FOKKER, EU DEFENCE ADVISER, 2008**

This is what I saw over the school in 1995

DATA TAKEN FROM MINISTRY OF ALIEN DEFENCE RECORDS 1989-2014

MINISTRY OF ALIEN DEFENCE

ALIEN ABDUCTIONS

As with UFO sightings, only recently have we begun to gather statistics on what's now recognised to be a worldwide phenomenon – alien abduction. This is the taking of a human against his or her will to meet some kind of alien need, typically medical research. In this book we'll outline a whole range of tips and techniques to defend yourself against this very personal kind of invasion, but for now we'll take a quick look at the statistics. The number of people disappearing worldwide is at an all-time high. There's no single database, but the USA, Japan and Europe keep the best statistics.

▶ According to the charity Missing Persons, over 20,000 Britons vanish every year.
▶ In the USA, some 2,300 people vanish every day – there's no trace and they're never seen again. This excludes those who return within 48 hours of going missing.
▶ In Japan, since 2001, over 4,000,000 people have been reported to the police as missing.
▶ Over 100,000 people globally say they've been implanted with alien tracking devices or 'implants' – some of them are probably crazy, but all of them?

Some people, of course, change their identities, start a new life, fall down a well or just jump in the sea when their favourite sci-fi show is cancelled, but we're still looking at millions of people every year going missing and the evidence increasingly suggests that they're being taken by beings from beyond this Earth. And these reports aren't just restricted to Europe, North America and Japan. In 2005, General Wang Li-Cha of the People's Red Army in China reportedly told a US counterpart that no less than 42% of the Chinese cyber-defence budget was allocated to combating what he termed 'the saucer disappearances' and 'reptilian conspiracies'. According to Pentagon sources, the General reported that over 93,000 people had been taken by aliens in 2004 alone in the People's Republic of China and that it was on the agenda of the party, which considered the issue a threat to the nation.

" SINCE THE COLLAPSE OF THE US TREATY WITH THE GREYS IN 1980, IT'S BECOME OPEN SEASON ON EARTH, WITH THE NUMBER OF ABDUCTIONS GOING THROUGH THE ROOF. IF WE WERE HONEST WITH THE PUBLIC, WE'D HAVE TO SAY THAT WE'RE CURRENTLY POWERLESS TO STOP THESE SHIPS ENTERING OUR AIRSPACE AND KIDNAPPING CITIZENS AT WILL. "
MINISTRY OF DEFENCE BRIEFING, WHITEHALL, 2014

SO WHY NOW?

If aliens have been around for so many years, how is it that we're only now just beginning to see the scope and threat of extra-terrestrial intervention on our planet? Why didn't they just invade when we were at a much lower level of development?

It's a good question and in truth no-one is 100% sure. We know that aliens have attempted interventions on Earth before and some of these will be explored in later chapters. However, there are several factors in the past few decades that have made us a far more viable prospect for invasion.

MORE NOISE

Our noise level in the universe has greatly increased in the past 50 years – we've sent out into space everything from deep-space probes with our image and location to episodes of all the naff TV shows that have ever been made.

Add to this our rudimentary attempts at space travel and the creation and use of nuclear weapons, and you can see that our activities cannot have gone unnoticed to species outside our solar system.

SEIZE THE DAY

The requirements of some potential invaders have changed. For example, the Greys have tried some form of dialogue with humanity to support their need for vast quantities of DNA and bio-matter, but for them talking simply hasn't delivered what they need. For others, such as the Draconians and Little Green Men, perhaps they see the present as the opportune time to invade – before we develop any further.

ALIENS – FACT OR FICTION?

GREAT ALIEN MYTHS

By now you should be convinced that there are envious alien eyes watching our planet very closely and working on their invasion plans. However, this doesn't mean that every negative thing happening on Earth is down to extra-terrestrial visitors. In this section we debunk some of the widely held misconceptions about aliens. It's vital that we all focus on our real objective, which is to prevent a takeover of Earth by alien forces rather than spend months trying to prove that a weird circle in the cornfields of Wiltshire was caused by a rogue X-wing fighter.

Any search on the internet will uncover hundreds of myths relating to alien intervention on Earth. While there's some truth hidden among the many web pages of fiction, it's often hard to tell one from the other. This section, therefore, will focus on the most pervasive myths around extra-terrestrials – we'll leave out the most fantastical stuff. We should also inject a note of caution: in this field what can at first sound bizarre may one day turn out to be the truth. So here's what we know for sure – so far!

MYTH 1
ALIENS ARE CAUSING GLOBAL CLIMATE CHANGE

Some people say that Earth is getting hotter, others that it's getting colder. The reptiles prefer it warm, so they must be heating up the planet; the Greys like it cool, so it must be them cooling it down. Nothing divides alien watchers and conspiracy theorists more than the controversy of climate change. There's no doubt that species such as the Draconians would prefer a warmer Earth and there's some evidence that they're linked to some of the world's biggest CO_2 polluting companies. As for other species, we have no real proof that they're purposely manipulating our environment. This doesn't mean that species such as the Little Green Men won't get busy 'terra-forming' once they actually invade, but for the moment the quantity of greenhouse gases we're pumping into the Earth's atmosphere is all our own work.

MYTH 2
ALIENS ARE RESPONSIBLE FOR CROP CIRCLES

Crop circles are the biggest hoax in alien investigations and more words have been wasted on them than on, for example, practical military plans for the defence of our planet. At a rough count, there are over 4,000 books on the subject, with theories ranging from how they're created by gods to suggestions that they're messages from aliens trying to make contact. In the very real world of alien defence, the only 'crop circles' we recognise are the burn marks left by a Grey saucer. Whenever these ships or other space vessels land on the planet, they leave indentations, burns or scorch marks and, yes, crushed crops. Sometimes they're left in circular patterns, sometimes not. But we have no evidence that any species is trying to make contact by leaving odd shapes in our countryside.

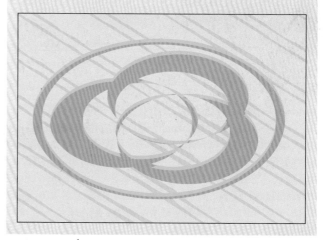

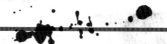

ALIENS – FACT OR FICTION?
THE RISE OF REALITY TV

May explain why the TV series Firefly was cancelled. Note to self to follow up

It may seem strange to readers that while classic TV series such as *Firefly* are cancelled, reality shows with their 'follow-a-nobody' formula are regularly getting into their fifth series. But does this rapid expansion of crap TV really mean that the cold, clammy hand of the alien invader is at work in TV studios? The simple answer is that we don't know. Media is certainly a useful way to reach the mass populace and billions of people around the world have access to TV, but we have no evidence at the moment that aliens are working to 'dumb down' our TV programmes and in the process dumbing down the IQ of the general populace.

Aliens would be better off spending their time damaging computer, engineering, maths and science education in schools and colleges, for these are the disciplines we need to meet the technological challenges that lie ahead.

> **IT HAS BEEN ESTIMATED THAT THE AVERAGE ADULT WILL LOSE ONE IQ POINT FOR EVERY 20 HOURS OF REALITY TV WATCHED. THIS INCREASES TO TWO IQ POINTS IF THE SHOW INVOLVES A PHONE VOTE.**
> **WASHINGTON INSTITUTE OF EMPIRICAL RESEARCH**

MYTH 3
NEW-AGE CULTS ARE A GOOD WAY TO MEET ALIENS

There are several prominent quasi-religious organisations around the world that cite contact with extra-terrestrials as one of their 'membership benefits'. Invariably, any contact ends up costing a fortune and several of these cults are now thriving, offering everything from a free half-consultation with a Grey to guaranteed rescues in an alien ship when the world ends. Alien visitors have had contact from time to time with religious leaders in the past but most of this contact by far has been through the Nordics via Buddhist monks in Tibet and India. While other alien species struggle to get their very different minds around human religion, the Nordics have engaged in open dialogue with those they perceive as enlightened. This doesn't extend to the locally produced monthly DVDs for just $15.99 on subscription.

Speak to Father Ulich about this – not mentioned during Mass

MYTH 4
SO, WHAT'S GOING ON WITH THE BEES?

There has been a suspected link between aliens and bees since the 1970s and many conspiracy theorists have pointed to the potentially disastrous collapse in pollinator numbers as evidence of an alien conspiracy at work. The often-cited hypothesis is that the Greys have manipulated bee DNA in an effort to either spread 'rogue DNA' throughout our ecosystem or as part of their own DNA-splicing trials. Wilder theories suggest that alien invaders are attacking our ecosystem by stealth, by destroying some of the key pillars of nature such as pollination. The TV series ▓▓▓▓▓▓ played very much on the fear that aliens were experimenting with bees. Those patient enough to follow this long-running series were further confused when it linked bees with a plan to spread a virus among the human population.

ALIENS – FACT OR FICTION?

THE UK PERSPECTIVE

Although the facts contained in this volume have been gathered from international sources, the Ministry of Alien Defence (MAD) in London is charged with protecting the UK population and airspace from the extra-terrestrial threat. The office was created in 1981 following events in the USA; prior to this alien threats had been managed and investigated by the RAF. The MAD now fields a force of over 200 managers and 50 Men in Black investigation teams. The Extra-Terrestrial Security Act 1979 defines our role as being:

> **THE PROTECTION OF NATIONAL SECURITY AND, IN PARTICULAR, ITS PROTECTION AGAINST THREATS FROM ABDUCTION, IMPLANTS AND LIVESTOCK MUTILATION, FROM THE ACTIVITIES OF AGENTS OF ALIEN POWERS, AND FROM ACTIONS INTENDED TO UNDERMINE PARLIAMENTARY DEMOCRACY BY POLITICAL, INDUSTRIAL OR VIOLENT MEANS.**
> **THE EXTRA-TERRESTRIAL SECURITY ACT**

IN PURSUING THE ROLE SET OUT BY THE ACT, THE CORPORATE AIMS OF THE MINISTRY OF ALIEN DEFENCE ARE:

- Frustrate alien intervention.
- Prevent damage to the UK from alien espionage and other covert alien activity.
- Foster the procurement of alien material, technology or expertise relating to weapons or propulsion.
- Watch out for new or re-emerging types of alien threats, particularly around cloning.
- Protect Government's sensitive information and assets, and the Critical National Infrastructure (CNI).
- Assist the Secret Intelligence Service (SIS) and the Government Communications Headquarters (GCHQ) in the discharge of their statutory functions.
- Build resilience to a possible invasion from outer space and management of the UK's Men in Black resources.
- Work with the United Nations Office for Earth Defence.

ALIENS – FACT OR FICTION?
THE UK'S MEN IN BLACK

Tales of UFO witnesses and abductees being visited by 'Men in Black' date back as far as the 1830s in the USA. They have often been seen as part of some sinister plot by the government to silence people on the alien threat to Earth or, worse still, as part of the extra-terrestrial invasion itself. However, for the Men in Black operating in the UK today, nothing could be further from the truth.

EYE-WITNESS ACCOUNT

Peggy Moore, 89, from Grasslands Nursing Home has been abducted over 100 times in her lifetime. She's seen how the Men in Black have changed their approach over the years.

> **THE GRILLING THE AGENTS GAVE ME WHEN I RETURNED WAS WORSE THAN THE ABDUCTION ITSELF. THEY ASKED ALL KINDS OF QUESTIONS, BANGING THE TABLE WHEN I DIDN'T ANSWER MUCH. AND, WOE BETIDE IF YOU DIDN'T REPORT IT. NOW IT'S DIFFERENT. YOU CAN BOOK AN APPOINTMENT WITH THEM ONLINE AND THEY'RE VERY POLITE.**
> **PEGGY MOORE, 100+ ALIEN ABDUCTIONS**

No mention of rapping skills – this is good news!

FACTS ABOUT MEN IN BLACK UNITS IN THE UK

- A Men in Black unit is typically made up of 2–3 special agents, with one being office-based at any one time.
- The term 'Men in Black' is no longer used within the Ministry of Alien Defence, the teams being referred to as Extra-Terrestrial Investigation Units (ETIU).
- Over 54% of Men in Black are in fact female and very few agents actually wear black. In addition, few wear sunglasses due to health and safety concerns.
- Recruitment of Men in Black is generally via other UK, Irish, American or Commonwealth security agencies.
- Men in Black are officially categorised as 'civil servants'. Their role sounds exciting – in 2013 they filed over 6,000 UFO sighting and abduction reports – but they are in fact as skilled in paperwork as they are with ray guns!
- Like MI5 and MI6 agents, investigators working for the Ministry of Alien Defence carry the same authority in law as a senior police inspector. In other words, they have an official badge that enables them to enter any location where they have suspicions that a 'crime' is taking place. Most are licensed to carry firearms or other 'high-tech' weapons.

ALIEN KNOWLEDGE 101

If you've read this far, you should now be convinced of the real threat to our planet. There are aliens out there – fact. Tens of thousands of humans are being abducted every year – fact. Our planet is woefully unprepared to face any invasion – fact.

For those new to these facts, it can all be a bit overwhelming. One immediately starts thinking about sending cash to NASA or wearing a tin-foil hat when outdoors. Later we'll look at all the skills you need to consider yourself an 'ET prepper' – someone who's fully prepared to combat and resist all forms of alien invasion. But the first step to defending our planet is knowledge.

The term 'alien' describes every species other than humanity but this group is far from homogenous, with different physiology, social structure and even chemical make-up. In fact, we now know that there are millions of different species out there – currently the Ministry of Alien Defence recognises around <u>300 different life forms and they all have different drivers, motives and game plans.</u>

DRIVERS FOR INVASION

Assessing alien drivers for invasion is a bit like asking why humans fight wars on Earth – in reality it's a complex mix of greed, jealousy, empire building, scientific curiosity and even species eradication. Every alien species out there will have its own unique needs and pressures.

Over the years organisations have used various descriptions to categorise the invasion motives of aliens – terms include destroyers, imperial powers, scavengers, re-locators, raiders and crusaders. All of this caused significant confusion among the alien-watching community, so in 2006 the Ministry of Alien Defence started working with the United Nations Organisation for Earth Defence on a unified classification of alien invasion motives. Was that meeting as interesting as it sounds? The outcomes are presented on the facing page.

ALIEN KNOWLEDGE 101
WHY HAVE YOU COME TO EARTH?

The website wiki-alieninvasion.com claims that 42 alien ships have crashed on Earth since 1912, leaving 17 survivors representing at least four different species. By hacking into top-secret documents around the world, the website claims that it can reveal the answer to the real question we want to ask – why have you come to Earth?

SHOULD WE BELIEVE THIS SURVEY?
Well, it's the only one of its kind ever attempted and although we cannot validate the sources, the survey seems to suggest that in the past we had more positive interactions with alien species – and we do know that since the 1980s we have had very little positive communication with alien species. This suggests that those species that do 'want to get to know us' have been driven away or have left the scene, leaving us open to the more hostile varieties. The results have been moderated against a scale as communication has not always been in an Earth language and not all aliens could answer the question.

It sounded like a laugh

Do not trust wiki-alieninvasion.com – the founder is currently sheltering in the Venezuelan embassy after clocking up hundreds of unpaid parking tickets

I'm below probing quota

We bring great advances in science and medicine

We find your planet and species of interest and have come to observe

We need more food so have come to raid your planet for resources

$$x = (-1)^n \arcsin \frac{1}{2} + \pi_n = (-1)^n \frac{\pi}{6}$$
$$x = \pm \arccos \frac{\sqrt{2}}{2} + 2\pi_n = \pm \frac{\pi}{4} + 2$$
$$x = \arctan \sqrt{3} + \pi_n = \frac{\pi}{3} + \pi_{n \sin^2}$$

To rid the Earth of the human vermin. Your very existence is offensive to my species!

SOURCE: VARIOUS NATIONAL GOVERNMENT RECORDS AND THE WASHINGTON MEMORANDUM, VOL. IX

▶ ALIEN MOTIVATION MATRIX

In 2008 the United Nations Organisation for Earth Defence agreed an Alien Motivation Matrix that's now used world-wide to help develop plans to manage and combat any hostile alien intervention on Earth or within our solar system.

The Matrix is far from perfect and it's immediately clear how these basic categories can overlap and change over time. They must also be considered alongside the capacity of an alien species to invade Earth. For example, a species limited to a few hundred beings will be unlikely to want to risk a ground offensive on the planet and, despite its advanced technology, may not be able to complete a takeover, preferring instead to use more subtle means.

CLASSIFICATION	KEY FEATURES, VECTORS & METHODS	EXAMPLES FROM KNOWN SPECIES
1 OBSERVERS	Very low probability of hostile intervention. Possible avoidance of contact altogether. May be operating under a *Star Trek* type 'prime directive' of non-intervention. There's a risk that this category could move into a judgement phase in which assessment is made of humanity's right to exist.	▶ **The Nordics** ▶ **Species 1009 – AA** (gaseous life form with no name) ▶ **Species 1011 – HH** (known as future humans)
2 SCIENTISTS EXPLORERS	Humanity can expect an increased level of contact and intervention. Some may have the basic agenda of a quest for knowledge. Intervention to meet an objective is acceptable but typically wouldn't involve a planetary invasion. The species may attempt to manipulate humanity from the background or support our ongoing development.	▶ **Greys up to 1979** ▶ **Draconians at various times in history** ▶ **Species 282 – CC** (known as 'Horned Greys') ▶ **Species 213 – CC** (known as 'Space Pixies')
3 INVADERS OCCUPIERS SETTLERS	This category sees Earth as a potential home world and could come either in peace or as would-be conquerors. Motivations may include a dying home planet or just empire growth. Alien refugees from an inter-galactic war may also fall into this category. This category will have a profound impact on humanity and most scientists agree that any intervention will be hostile.	▶ **Little Green Men** ▶ **Draconians** ▶ ▬▬▬▬▬
4 SCAVENGERS	Earth and its resources, including humanity and the incredible diversity of bio-matter, will be of interest to many scavengers. For example, humans may be taken from the planet to become part of a slave labour force. Although an unremarkable planet in terms of minerals and ores, Earth has elements that are considered valuable elsewhere in the universe.	▶ **Greys after 1979** ▶ **Little Green Men in some scenarios** ▶ **Species 441 – DD** (known as 'Rigelians')
5 EXTERMINATORS	This is an extremely hostile category. With various motivations, exterminators have a mission to extinguish life on Earth. Maybe they will become new occupiers, but occupation will be preceded by the eradication of all human life. Currently, we only know of one species with this agenda and this is only applicable under specific conditions around the movement of their home world. But there are others out there who see any species different from their own as a nuisance to be destroyed, much as one might think nothing of wiping out a colony of pesky ants.	▶ **Insectoids** (known as 'The Species') *Caught a spider looking at me strangely yesterday but he's an arachnid – does that count?*

ALIEN KNOWLEDGE 101

ALIENS IN JUDGEMENT

In extra-terrestrial defence circles, they call it the Roffey Syndrome, after the Oxford scientist Steve Roffey who first theorised it back in 1978. Having spent time in Tibet and having witnessed a Nordic visitation, Dr Roffey was the first to link the disappearance of alien worlds with the existence of superbeings who may arrive, sit in judgement, then decide the fate of a species.

DR STEVE ROFFEY

'I completed my research in the summer of 1977, noting with some interest that the Perilo system in an outer quadrant had disappeared. I mentioned this to the milkman but he seemed most disinterested. It was not until I was privileged enough to hear the Nordics speaking in Tibet that I realised just how vulnerable we are to their strong moralistic line of questioning. I was able to ask one of the aliens if it knew anything about the disappearance. It looked sheepish and promptly dematerialised.'

Roffey went on to suggest that some species may develop to such a degree that they feel they are able to sit in judgement over what they see as lesser species. We have no evidence that the Nordics fit into this category but we have prepared some guidelines as follows.

▶ OUR AMAZING PLANET

If you're approached by any form of superbeing asking you to make a case for humanity's survival, think very carefully before deciding whether you're best qualified to answer the question on behalf of the billions on the planet. If you decide you are, try to relax and take the superbeing through the amazing things about our planet and people. Mention the wonderful bio-diversity on Earth; leave out any extinctions and if necessary say they were dead when we got here.

▶ DON'T MENTION THE WARS!

Steer the focus away from any war or conflict. If they ask, just infer that we've had a few 'fall-outs' from time to time but on the whole we're a peaceful and curious species.

▶ DON'T UNDERWHELM THEM!

Don't rush to locations such as Stonehenge as there's a danger that a superbeing will be distinctly underwhelmed by our ability to put large stones on top of each other. In terms of other locations to show any aliens who stand in judgement over humanity, try Venice (out of season), Harvard or any great sporting events. Avoid New York in the summer, war zones or Oxford Street in London.

▶ ACT SMART!

Don't get drawn into any discussion on time dilation, string theory or why they cancelled the TV series *Firefly*. One day mankind may understand these things but as yet they're beyond our intelligence. It may be worth learning a few clever quips in binary as that always goes down well.

⚠ IF ALL ELSE FAILS
USE SIMPLE BUT CONFUSING RIDDLES

'WHY DID THE CHICKEN CROSS THE ROAD?'
'TO GET TO THE OTHER SIDE.'
Once you've delivered your punch line, pause and raise your eyebrows as if you're trying to confirm that the superbeing has understood. The trick is to hint that there's some deep meaning. In some instances, a superbeing may well see something that we don't.

 MINISTRY OF ALIEN DEFENCE

ALIEN TECHNOLOGY MATRIX

Planners love a matrix and as soon as the Alien Motivation Matrix was completed a technology one was promptly tabled. On a serious note, it's important in any military assessment that both intent and capability are assessed, and the Alien Technology Matrix below was added to the Alien Motivation Matrix in 2009 after a seriously long meeting. After all, there may be millions of hostile alien civilisations out there in the universe but many won't have the technologies to wage war, while others may lack the power-creation expertise to devise an inter-stellar propulsion system. The table below summarises our current knowledge about known alien species.

LIFE FORM	SPACE TRAVEL	SOLAR SYSTEM TRAVEL	GALAXY TRAVEL	UNIVERSE TRAVEL	DIMENSIONAL TRAVEL	EXAMPLES FROM KNOWN SPECIES
T0 MICROBIAL LIFE	✓ On solar winds/asteroids	✓	✗	✗	✗	▶ Space fungus ▶ Draconian fungus
T1 PRE-INDUSTRIAL LIFE	✗	✗	✗	✗	✗	▶ Species 611 – AA
T2 CIVILISATION (NON-SPACE)	✗	✗	✗	✗	✗	▶ Species 678 – HH
T3 TERRAN NORMAL	✓	✗	✗	✗	✗	▶ Current Earth
T4 SOLAR SYSTEM COLONISERS	✓	✓	✗	✗	✗	▶ Earth plus 100 years ▶ Species 441 – DD ▶ The Skulkrin Imperium
T5 GALACTIC MOVERS	✓	✓	✓	✗	✗	▶ Greys/Little Green Men ▶ Species 282 – CC 'Horned Greys' ▶ Species 213 – CC 'Space Pixies'
T6 UNIVERSE MOVERS	✓	✓	✓	✓	✗	▶ Draconians ▶ Insectoids
T7 GOD-LIKE ABILITIES	✓	✓	✓	✓	✓	▶ Nordics ▶ Mirror Men ▶ Species 1009 – AA Gaseous lifeform ▶ Species 1011 – HH 'future humans'

The lizards are already here! (handwritten note next to T6)

17

THE GREYS (ROSWELL GREYS, ZETANS)

The Greys are perhaps the most recognisable aliens for most of humanity due to their portrayal in cinema and fiction and, in particular, the popular *X-Files* series of the 1990s. With this in mind, there are more misconceptions about the Greys than any other species, with significant confusion around both their motivation and their level of contact with the human race. Many alien watchers believe that the Greys are the only extra-terrestrials to have visited Earth and see them as a paternal influence, guiding humankind, but as things stand at the moment the truth is far more sinister.

Initially the Greys – the only alien species with whom we have had formal and protracted contact – were regarded primarily as scientists and observers, but the past 50 years have seen a massive shift in our relationship with them and it has now broken down to the point where the Greys should be considered as potential invaders of our planet.

MOST EXPERTS NOW AGREE THAT THE GREYS' DESPERATION FOR BIO-DIVERSE MATTER AND THE FACT THAT THEIR SPECIES STANDS ON THE BRINK OF EXTINCTION MEAN THAT HUMANITY WILL FACE A GREY INVASION WITHIN THE NEXT 10–20 YEARS.

▶ APPEARANCE AND ABILITIES

WHAT WE KNOW!

The species known as the Greys comprises small humanoid life forms with an oversized head compared with human standards. We have little information on the natural lifespan of Grey individuals, but there's some evidence to indicate that a Grey transfers its mental intelligence into a new body once its existing body reaches a certain age.

In most of the human contact with Greys, only subtle differences have been observed between individuals, making it quite a challenge to tell them apart. Greys don't refer to themselves by any individual name.

HEIGHT	1–1.5 metres
WEIGHT	20–40kg
COLOUR	Pallid grey colour with a damp texture
LIKES	Pasta, sneezing and cats
DISLIKES	Snooker and backwards running

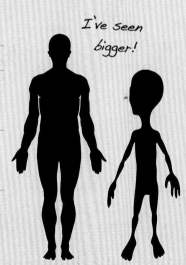

I've seen bigger!

PHYSICAL FEATURES

▶ Bones are thin but very flexible, being made of malleable cartilage. Greys may have adapted their bodies to cope with the demands of space travel.

▶ Eyes are large, black and slanting upwards, with very thin 'eyelids' that rarely seem to close. Grey eyes are particularly sensitive to fine particles such as dust.

▶ Greys have long arms that end in long, slender fingers; each hand has three fingers and a thin thumb. Although not every Grey alien is exactly the same, the ratio between height, arm and leg length is always the same, hinting that each Grey, in fact, is a clone – although the species allows for some diversity.

▶ Lack of any sexual organs. Greys are asexual and have no concept of male and female.

▶ A Grey has a small mouth and tiny airways instead of a nose. Greys can breathe Earth's atmosphere but appear very sensitive to pollution.

ABILITIES

▶ Greys have strong telepathic abilities and rarely emit any noise from their mouths. They have the ability to engage in regular communication through telepathy but also to aggressively plant concepts into their victims' brains and even control their will and movement. They can create a neural network that enables them to share knowledge between themselves.

ALIEN KNOWLEDGE 101
THE GREY AGENDA

The Greys are primarily interested in both human DNA and the wider bio-diversity of our planet. The Greys are master manipulators of DNA and evolution, thousands of years ahead of anything we can conceive, but this hasn't stopped them leading their species into an evolutionary dead end. We have documented evidence that the Greys switched long ago to cloning to reproduce and that this technology worked for them for tens of thousands of years. We also suspect that they've spliced alien DNA into their own at various points in their history. However, they now face a major crisis for reasons even they cannot fathom: their clones are increasingly weak and unable to survive. Hence, for much of the 20th century and onwards, the Greys looked to Earth to satisfy their need for bio-diversity. ██████████████████████████

██████████████████████████ *08/02 hg*

This guy starred in Close Encounters of the Third Kind, The X-Files and Stargate. He must have a good agent.

ALIEN MOTIVATION MATRIX: 2/4
SCIENTISTS OR SCAVENGERS?

With the breakdown of the Greys' treaty with humanity in 1979, their agenda has shifted to one of resource collection. They are, therefore, now classed as a scavenger species. They are interested in DNA and bio-matter of all descriptions and so we must assume they that would be prepared to strip our planet and leave it a sterile, lifeless rock if it ensured that their species could survive.

ALIEN TECHNOLOGY MATRIX: T5
GALACTIC MOVERS

The Greys are experienced space travellers but haven't yet traversed the whole universe. Distance is a factor for this species and it will impact on any Earth-invasion strategy. For example, it'll take time for the Greys to bring in any reinforcements. However, despite all of their technological knowledge, Grey civilisation is facing the threat of extinction due to the gradual degradation of their DNA material.

Greys are asexual so what are Haynes trying to hide?

THE GREYS ARE DESPERATE TO SOLVE THEIR CLONING CRISIS AND SEE THE RICH BIO-MASS OF EARTH AS THE BEST CHANCE THEY HAVE OF SAVING THEIR OWN SPECIES. FROM THEIR VIEWPOINT, THEY'VE TRIED TALKING AND IT HASN'T WORKED, SO HUMANITY MUST BE PREPARED FOR A MAJOR GREY INVASION IN THE NEAR FUTURE.

TECHNOLOGY

Known as a Type 1 Grey Saucer, this type of ship has been spotted over Earth countless times. Finally, one crashed in Roswell, New Mexico in 1947 and has been reverse-engineered for over 50 years.

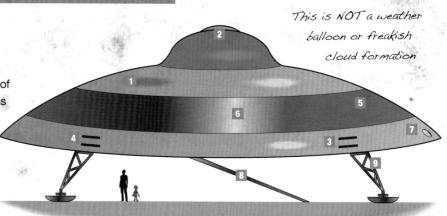

This is NOT a weather balloon or freakish cloud formation

1. Silver non-reflective metal (unknown).
2. Metal dome housing the Command Bridge.
3. Shield nodes around the vessel, generating a powerful protective shield (energy type unknown).
4. Energy pulse weapons (can be used in atmosphere or space).
5. Rotating band believed to be linked to the ship's gravitational propulsion system.
6. A wide strip of moving metallic liquid that pulsates when the ship is in flight – known as 'the glowing band'.
7. Tractor beam – used for abductions and capable of lifting many hundreds of tonnes.
8. Retractable landing stairs.
9. Landing struts.
10. Sealed hyper-drive unit.
11. Propulsion unit (anti-gravity).
12. Liquid display linked to ship's systems.
13. Bio-computers, with bio-engineered 'processing units'.
14. Bio-mass that feeds into the ship.
15. Operation table.
16. Experimentation chamber – the location is familiar to millions of abduction victims around the world.
17. Cryogenic chambers for samples.
18. Tractor beam hatchway.
19. Sealed pods, purpose unknown.
20. Escape saucer – there's one of these mini-saucers in Area 51 but it hasn't been possible to activate it.
21. Sleep booths that double as cryogenic pods for crew members.
22. Command bridge.
23. Biological computer and controls.
24. Five flight seats.
25. Flight control method is unclear; theorised to be a neural link.

MAIN DECK

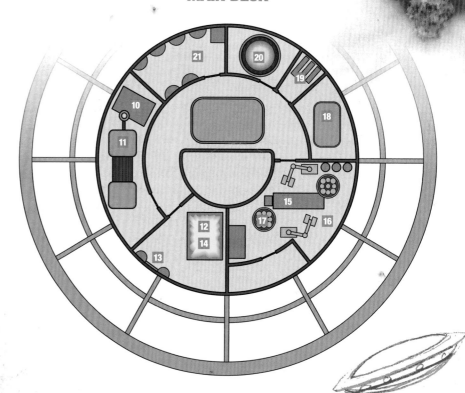

COMMAND BRIDGE

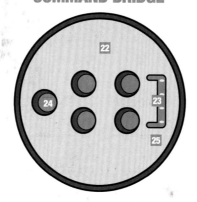

> DESPITE HAVING ACCESS TO A CRASHED TYPE 1, TO HUNDREDS OF DEBRIS PARTS AND HAVING THE EXPERIENCE OF SENDING HUMANS ON BOARD GREY VESSELS DURING THE TIME OF THE GREADA TREATY, WE ARE STILL A LONG WAY FROM UNDERSTANDING THE PHYSICS AND DYNAMICS OF THESE SHIPS.
> **UNNAMED SOURCE 244, AREA 51**

MINISTRY OF ALIEN DEFENCE

SOCIETY *Say 'no' to alien abductions!*

The Greys have an egalitarian social structure, with no apparent ranks and little hierarchy. Even though humanity has spent far more time with this species than any other, we're still unsure as to their level of telepathic communication. For example, we know that they can read human minds and implant ideas or suggestions but we know little about the extent of the neural network that the Greys have established to link themselves together. Our current working hypothesis is that the Greys have some kind of implant that enables them to establish this mind link and that it has become their main path of communication.

With this in mind, we suspect the Greys' home world to be a very boring place. Everyone knows pretty much everything. Pub quizzes are a waste of time and card games pointless. The Greys come across as emotionless aliens and we expect this to be reflected in a society that's very sterile, ordered and balanced.

ORIGIN AND HOME WORLD

There's a fundamental disagreement on this subject. According to the Greys, their home system is Zeta Reticuli, a wide binary star system in the southern constellation of Reticulum. However, the Draconians insist that they genetically designed the Greys as a slave species eons ago and implanted this history. Greys regard this allegation as an illogical insult.

The Greys' quest for bio-matter has taken them across millions of galaxies as they search for the right DNA sequences they could use to repair their own failing strings. We know that they've experimented with hybridisation, trying to introduce new bio-matter into their lineage by selective breeding.

TYPE 2 SAUCERS
Since 1980, UFO watchers have reported the sighting of new, slightly larger saucers over Earth. Type 1 saucers are 40–50 metres across, whereas the new ships, known as Type 2s, are believed to measure well over 100 metres in diameter.

▶ FACT OR FICTION?

The Greys have been featured in more movies than any other species but often these portrayals have caused confusion among alien watchers across the globe. Here's a quick run-down of some of the most famous blurred lines between fact and fiction.

There was a government programme in *The X-Files* that allowed the Greys to abduct people.

FACT The Greys did in fact have a formal treaty with the American government until 1979 and under this treaty they were free to take a certain number of people providing they were returned.

The Greys are visitors who want to get to know us, like in *Close Encounters of the Third Kind*.

FICTION The Greys know humanity well enough and they've run out of time and patience with us. They've been aggressively abducting people for decades and now stand at the brink of a major invasion of the planet.

Greys look so sweet and helpless. They're actually rather cute, as in the movie *Paul*.

FICTION We wish this were the case. The movie *Paul* was hilarious but, in reality, the Greys have a far more sinister agenda. *Paul* was reasonably accurate in its physical portrayal of Greys, apart from the fact that they cannot dematerialise at will.

In the movie *Signs*, the Greys seem obsessed with making crop circles.

FICTION The Greys have never made crop circles. The only marks they leave behind are the burn marks from their saucer landings.

Is it true that there are Grey saucers hidden away in Area 51?

FACT There are many crashed alien ships around the world, including Grey saucers, but this doesn't mean that we understand all of the technology within such ships. Scientists have spent decades reverse-engineering these ships and we're just about getting to grips with some of the basics.

21

LITTLE GREEN MEN (LGM, MARTIANS)

After the Greys, Little Green Men (LGM) are probably the most recognisable alien species to the general populace. They were caricatured in countless pulp science fiction novels during the 1930s and 1940s and have frequently been referred to as Martians.

Little Green Men are an unpredictable and envious species of alien and this, combined with their passion for ray guns, makes them a particularly dangerous opponent for Earth. Their menacing, black, triangle-shaped ships have been seen countless times and files released after the fall of communism in East Germany prove conclusively that Little Green Men were working with the Nazi regime on their early jet fighters. Spiteful, vindictive and prone to vaporising things that irritate them, these aren't the sort of aliens with whom you'd want to be trapped in a lift.

THE LITTLE GREEN MEN ARE AN AMBITIOUS SPECIES, LOOKING TO EXPAND THEIR INFLUENCE ACROSS THE GALAXY. THEY MAY HAVE WHAT PSYCHOLOGISTS REFER TO AS AN 'INFERIORITY COMPLEX', AS THEY SHY AWAY FROM CONFLICT WITH THOSE THEY CONSIDER TO BE MORE TECHNOLOGICALLY ADVANCED, PREFERRING TO 'BULLY' SPECIES TO WHOM THEY FEEL SUPERIOR.

APPEARANCE AND ABILITIES

WHAT WE KNOW!

The species known as Little Green Men are diminutive humanoid life forms with a green hue to their skin. Little Green Men have typically been referred to as 'Martians' throughout history.

It's unlikely that Little Green Men would sit idly by as humanity develops deep-space travel and even faster-than-light capability. For this reason they're likely to become particularly dangerous to the planet during the 21st century.

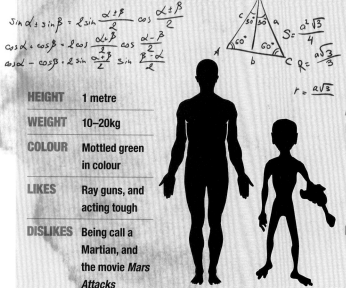

HEIGHT	1 metre
WEIGHT	10–20kg
COLOUR	Mottled green in colour
LIKES	Ray guns, and acting tough
DISLIKES	Being call a Martian, and the movie *Mars Attacks*

PHYSICAL FEATURES

▶ The species has been seen wearing space suits and sometimes a light form of chain-mail armour.

▶ Physically weak in comparison to humans, they're known to carry small ray guns, which can be lethal.

▶ They're full of bravado when armed and in company with their fellow aliens, but if found alone or injured at a crash site they adopt an almost child-like persona.

▶ Skin is a mottled green colour and said to be cool and textured to the touch. They sweat profusely when enraged – which is often – and the tops of their bald green heads are said to pulsate as they fume.

▶ Eyes are bulbous, with awhite background and black pupils. Frequently the eyes appear bloodshot and probably have significant blood vessels around them.

ABILITIES

▶ They have some telepathic abilities but can also communicate verbally in what, to humans, sounds like a constant and piercing stream of high-pitched banter. Witnesses have reported hearing words that sound like 'yak' and 'tak', and it seems that their language is made up entirely of variations on this theme.

▶ Part of the repertoire of the Little Green Men's speech lies in its rhythm and pitch. Orders are given at louder volume, while speeding up and higher pitch indicate irritation; a squealing 'laughter' sound has even been noted.

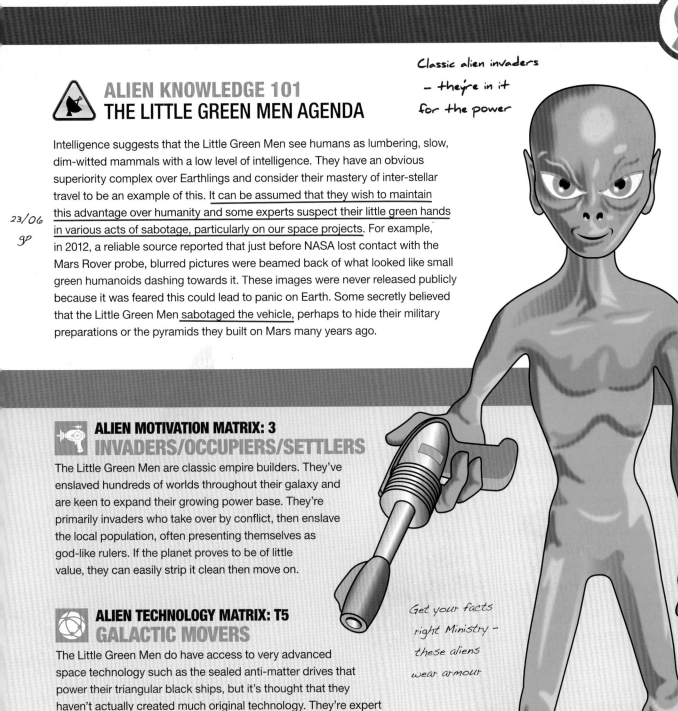

ALIEN KNOWLEDGE 101
THE LITTLE GREEN MEN AGENDA

Classic alien invaders – they're in it for the power

Intelligence suggests that the Little Green Men see humans as lumbering, slow, dim-witted mammals with a low level of intelligence. They have an obvious superiority complex over Earthlings and consider their mastery of inter-stellar travel to be an example of this. It can be assumed that they wish to maintain this advantage over humanity and some experts suspect their little green hands in various acts of sabotage, particularly on our space projects. For example, in 2012, a reliable source reported that just before NASA lost contact with the Mars Rover probe, blurred pictures were beamed back of what looked like small green humanoids dashing towards it. These images were never released publicly because it was feared this could lead to panic on Earth. Some secretly believed that the Little Green Men sabotaged the vehicle, perhaps to hide their military preparations or the pyramids they built on Mars many years ago.

23/06 gp

ALIEN MOTIVATION MATRIX: 3
INVADERS/OCCUPIERS/SETTLERS

The Little Green Men are classic empire builders. They've enslaved hundreds of worlds throughout their galaxy and are keen to expand their growing power base. They're primarily invaders who take over by conflict, then enslave the local population, often presenting themselves as god-like rulers. If the planet proves to be of little value, they can easily strip it clean then move on.

ALIEN TECHNOLOGY MATRIX: T5
GALACTIC MOVERS

The Little Green Men do have access to very advanced space technology such as the sealed anti-matter drives that power their triangular black ships, but it's thought that they haven't actually created much original technology. They're expert looters and avoid conflict with more advanced species such as the Draconians. The Little Green Men have invaded many worlds and have developed a range of specialised weapons, such as giant tripods, to support their domination of technologically inferior species.

Get your facts right Ministry – these aliens wear armour

GREY INTELLIGENCE SUGGESTS THAT THEY FREQUENTLY ARRIVE AS MILITARY CONQUERORS, PREFERRING TO USE LOCAL ELITES TO DIVIDE AND RULE THE PLANET. IN SOME CASES, THEY INSTALL THEMSELVES AS RATHER SMALL GODS.

⚙ TECHNOLOGY

A black triangle ship isn't detectable by radar and has the ability to change direction and speed in an instant. It's one of the most frequently spotted alien ships over Earth, most typically found around military installations and air bases.

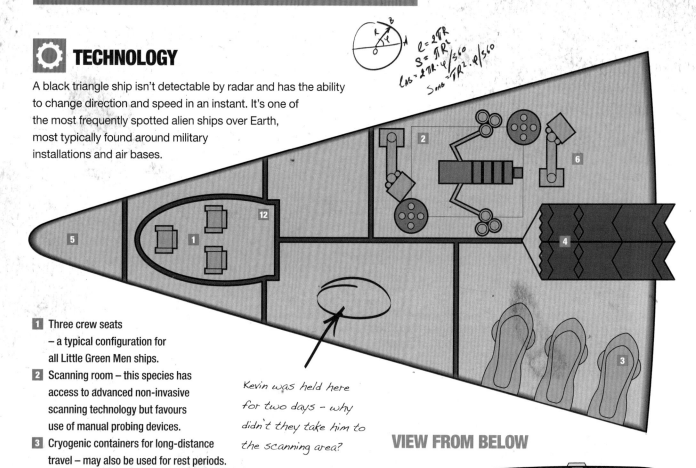

Kevin was held here for two days – why didn't they take him to the scanning area?

VIEW FROM BELOW

1. **Three crew seats** – a typical configuration for all Little Green Men ships.
2. **Scanning room** – this species has access to advanced non-invasive scanning technology but favours use of manual probing devices.
3. **Cryogenic containers** for long-distance travel – may also be used for rest periods.
4. **Sealed engine unit**, thought to be a small anti-matter drive.
5. **Internal gravitational unit** – it's thought that this unit enables the aliens to withstand the immense gravitational pull of their instant airborne changes of flight path.
6. **Cluttered Interior** – despite the smooth appearance on the outside, the interior of a black triangle ship is cluttered, with pieces of kit and technology wired in and clearly mismatched; black sticky tape is widely used to secure cables.
7. **Covered in black stealth tiles** – this technology has been successfully used by the Americans on their stealth programme and it's believed that the tiles are primarily designed to make the ship 'invisible' in space.
8. **Three external light sources.**
9. **Outside thrusters** enable this vessel to move in any direction.
10. **Laser nodes** on each corner of the ship enable it to fire high-energy beams in any direction. Typically these are set to fire in pulsating bursts.
11. **An electric kettle** – both crashed ships were found to have electric kettles from Earth. If the Little Green Men see technology they like, they have no problems just blending it with their own. In this case, something about the primitive heating element of an electric kettle attracted them.

THE POWER OF THREE

Typically black triangle ships fly in groups of three and in a tight holding pattern. This has confused some witnesses who believed that they were seeing one ship when in fact there were three of them.

SOCIETY

The object I saw on the way back from the pub was triangular

Little Green Men are known to be ambitious, devious and sometimes irrational. They're curious by nature but have no interest in inter-species communication unless it directly benefits them. They can appear child-like, selfish and even mischievous, delighting in matching any human achievements such as high-speed flight and interfering with any human space programme.

We know little of how Little Green Men society works. Evidence of their behaviour on Earth hints that they have a strict hierarchical structure but one that doesn't prevent an almost constant state of argument, debate and heated discussion. <u>The aliens appear to have a warrior class and it is believed that these are the only Little Green Men that humans have ever encountered.</u>

Little Green Men are scavengers of other technology and seem to have no concept of 'theft' when taking individuals or technology from other worlds. They study humanity purely from the viewpoint of what they can get out of it. Little Green Men are fond of weapons and individuals are rarely seen without their almost stereotypical 'ray gun'.

ORIGIN AND HOME WORLD

While the Little Green Men have been known to operate from a base on Mars, there has always been some confusion as to the origin of this species. In fact, they originate from near a pulsar known as PSR B1919+21 (or CP1919 as it was previously called) in the constellation of Vulpecula. This system is over 2,200 light years away and as such LGM ships require vast sources of energy to cover such distances.

The species has used its base on Mars to monitor Earth and several other planets of interest in nearby systems. In fact, it's thought that the recent attention of the Greys was one of the factors in the Little Green Men deciding to reopen their Mars site.

> ❝ THREE IS A NUMBER OF PARTICULAR RELEVANCE TO LITTLE GREEN MEN, ALTHOUGH WE DON'T KNOW WHY. ALL OF THE SHIPS HAVE SOME FORM OF TRIANGULAR SHAPE. MANY HAVE THREE PROMINENT LIGHTS. THE CREW OF THEIR SMALLER VESSELS IS THREE AND THE SHIPS OFTEN FLY IN A 'V-FORMATION' OF THREE SHIPS. ONE THEORY LINKS THIS TO THEIR UNUSUAL PHYSIOLOGY, WHICH PROVIDES MANY OF THEIR INTERNAL ORGANS IN TRIPLICATE. ❞

UNNAMED SOURCE 247, AREA 51

▶ LITTLE GREEN MEN FACTS

WHY LITTLE GREEN MEN?
The term 'Little Green Men' was first coined over 100 years ago on Earth and is considered to be highly offensive to the species. The Little Green Men have watched a lot of Earth television as they study our civilisation, their favourite shows including the BBC TV series *Bargain Hunt* and the *Star Wars* movies. In their own language, which has a fiendishly complicated syntax, they refer to themselves as 'The Original and Great Master Species of the Galaxy who are Greatly Blessed by the Mighty Ones and who are Brave and have the Power of Three' – that's a rough translation. That's what Little Green Men call themselves; no-one else calls them that.

A RARE SPECIES
It's estimated that there are fewer than a billion Little Green Men in the universe, making them one of the rarest alien species we know of. It's thought that their constant infighting almost reduced their civilisation to rubble so they decided to start picking on weaker alien species instead.

NEITHER MALE NOR FEMALE
Autopsies on Little Green Men bodies from crash sites on Earth reveal that, in fact, they're neither male nor female, so their description is misleading. A grainy picture of a bloated body was shown to a Nordic contact in Tibet in 2003 as it was suspected that the Little Green Man concerned was of a bigger variety and possibly even a male. Instead, the Nordic just shrugged and hinted that this was simply a fat specimen of no sex.

THE GREYS LEAD THE WAY
Little Green Men avoid contact with other more advanced alien species. A phenomenon that has confused UFO hunters occurs when an abduction by Greys – with their distinct saucer ships – is followed soon after by an incident with a triangular Little Green Men ship. Experts suggest that the Little Green Men are fearful that the Greys are gaining some advantage through their human experimentation and frequently make follow-up visits to monitor anything of interest.

DRACONIANS (THE FIRST ONES, REPTILIANS)

If every alien invasion scenario was one involving flying saucers, ray guns and tripods, then we would certainly be clearer about the threat we face. We could spend all of our time and resources on the military defence of our planet. However, the universe is far more complicated than that and there are many species that see <u>stealth and deception</u> as better ways to take control of both the human population and the planet. Of all the covert enemies of this planet, the lizard-like Draconians are the most persistent and dangerous.

Any search on the internet will yields thousands of websites dedicated to what's often termed the 'lizard menace'. Many are wildly inaccurate, making all kinds of claims about these elusive aliens. Others just sound crazed and delusional, with accusations that all politicians on Earth, and even entire populations, have been replaced by Draconian shape-shifters or clones.

THE DRACONIANS ARE MASTERS OF MISINFORMATION AND WE NOW BELIEVE THAT THE ALIENS THEMSELVES WORK TO FUEL THESE RUMOURS AND ACTIVELY SUPPORT THE 'LUNATIC FRINGE' ON THE INTERNET. THE DRACONIANS ARE EXPERTS AT HIDING IN PLAIN SIGHT AND WILL DO ANYTHING TO KEEP THEIR MASTER PLAN UNDER WRAPS.

▶ APPEARANCE AND ABILITIES

WHAT WE KNOW!   *You know nothing!*

The species known as the Draconians refer to themselves as 'The First Ones' and are large, bipedal lizard-like creatures with prominent head ridges. To humans, their most startling aspect is the capability to change form or 'shape-shift'. This enables Draconians to mimic other species, which makes them particularly dangerous opponents. It's believed that other reptilian species have similar capabilities.

Draconians have perfected techniques in the power of suggestion and can exercise significant control over human minds.

Humans – you are a puny species!

HEIGHT	2–2.5 metres
WEIGHT	90–130kg
COLOUR	Brown, smooth and scaly in places
LIKES	Byzantine politics and reptile charities
DISLIKES	Open confrontation, smoking, mammals

PHYSICAL FEATURES

▶ Skin is scaly in places but is reported to be cool and smooth in other areas. It may be that a warrior class has developed armoured scales, with overlapping plates of hardened shell.

▶ Eyes are yellow with vertical black slits for pupils. They're said to move rapidly and can roll independently of each other – which humans find very unsettling.

▶ Draconians are able to breathe on Earth but are sensitive to many sprays such as perfumes and even smoke.

▶ They don't have ears in a human sense but 'hear' through vibrations. They're very sensitive in this respect and will often tilt their heads as they pick up movements far away.

▶ Draconian hands extend to two or three large fingers with claws at the end. The claws can grow up to 10cm but this length is considered 'uncouth' by the Draconians and many creatures file their claws.

ABILITIES

▶ Draconians are typically very powerful creatures. When angry, they can spit bile-like acid that will burn human skin.

▶ Most important of all, Draconians have the ability to 'shape-shift' into different forms. In the 1950s it was believed that some form of chemical release 'fooled' people into believing Draconians changed form, but then TV cameras captured some actual occurences and proved the phenomenon beyond doubt. Science is at a loss to explain the shape-shifting abilities of Draconians.

ALIEN KNOWLEDGE 101
THE DRACONIAN AGENDA

The Earth has almost mythical status in the minds of the Draconians following more than 1,000 years of patient observation and infiltration, and many now believe that they're gradually taking over the planet. Their end game is to control Earth and slowly transform it into the heavenly paradise they believe it once was. ████████████████████

12/08
rp

████████████████████
████████████████████

The Draconians aren't a cruel species but it's important to understand that they see humans as 'usurper ape-creatures' who have unfairly dominated a planet that rightfully belongs to the lizards.

ALIEN MOTIVATION MATRIX: 3
INVADERS/SETTLERS

The Draconians have their 'eyes on the prize' – which is the planet Earth. They don't necessarily want to eradicate all human life; they may keep us around as slaves. But their objective is clear and they're patient and persistent in their pursuit.

ALIEN TECHNOLOGY MATRIX: T6
UNIVERSE MOVERS

The Draconians are highly advanced technologically but, unlike the Greys, they haven't lost all of their emotional intelligence – which makes them formidable opponents. Planners by nature, they make use of their travel and cloning technology to slowly undermine humanity, preparing the way for a takeover, if possible with humanity knowing nothing about it until it's too late.

DINOSAURS DOMINATED OUR PLANET FOR MILLIONS OF YEARS SO IT ISN'T SCIENCE FICTION TO CONJECTURE THAT A LIZARD RACE WOULD RETURN TO TAKE THE EARTH AS ITS OWN.

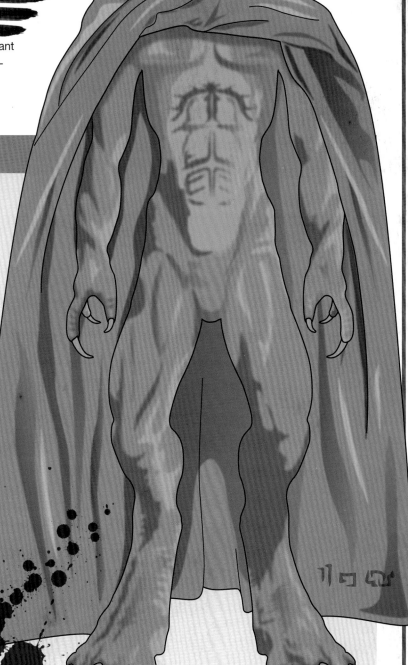

Is the weather girl on TV a shape-shifter? She was wearing a blue cloak the other day.

ALIEN KNOWLEDGE 101

⚙ TECHNOLOGY

The Draconian 'pod ship' is designed for stealth and to conceal itself on alien worlds. In the absence of a more secure base, it provides numerous 'pods' via which Draconians can clone alien life forms and infiltrate their societies.

Pod ships have only rarely been caught on camera and are equipped with powerful stealth technology that seems to create the illusion of being able to see through a vessel.

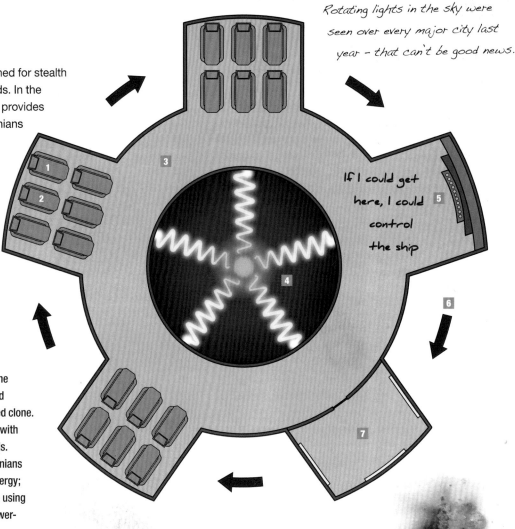

Rotating lights in the sky were seen over every major city last year – that can't be good news.

If I could get here, I could control the ship

1. Each hub is populated with clone pods that double up as sleep or rest chambers.
2. Each cloning requires three pods: one for a Draconian, one for the captured human and one for the manufactured clone.
3. The interior is surprisingly Spartan, with no decoration and few control panels.
4. The Central Energy Hub – the Draconians have access to vast resources of energy; scientists believe that the aliens are using some form of trans-dimensional power-generating capability.
5. Navigation hub.
6. Ship spins rapidly in flight.
7. Abduction Room – the function of this room is uncertain, although some sources suggest that it's used for abductions and implants.
8. Reflective tiles give an illusion of invisibility.
9. When landed, the ship generates a powered stealth field.
10. Pod ships are designed to spend long periods of time 'cloaked' – almost invisible.
11. Pod cruisers are said to be between 50 and 100 metres in diameter.
12. The landing struts on a pod ship contain long root-like metal tendrils that reach down into a planet; it's believed that these are used to extract water or perhaps geo-thermal energy.

> DRACONIANS MAKE USE OF NANO-TECHNOLOGY TO MONITOR HUMANITY, DEPLOYING THE MOST ADVANCED IMPLANT TECHNOLOGY EVER SEEN. THEY HAVE BEEN SEEN USING SMALL WRIST DEVICES FOR VARIOUS ACTIVITIES SUCH AS LOCATION TRACKING.
> **TECHNOLOGY ADVISER, UK CABINET BRIEFING, 2013**

THE CLOAKED SHIP
You can sometimes catch a glimpse of a cloaked vessel as it will occasionally shimmer, particularly in smoky conditions.

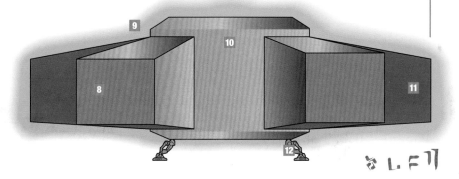

 MINISTRY OF ALIEN DEFENCE

SOCIETY

Draconians are highly political creatures, living in very structured, ordered societies in which a slight mispronunciation can result in deep offence and shunning. Their approach to all things is typically indirect. They'll avoid direct confrontation where possible, preferring the Byzantine approaches of infiltration, conspiracy and control by proxy. For example, as hatchlings they're encouraged to engage in fiendishly complex and cruel mind games with the rest of their brood, with the most influential 'child' becoming the favoured one.

They greatly value power over just wealth and firmly believe that humans are a second-class species. Something Draconians often point out is how humans kill each other. In Draconian society, killing another lizard is strictly taboo. However, they think nothing of eating their young if the hatchlings don't come up to standard, so they shouldn't be too judgemental just because some humans like a bit of 'rough and tumble'.

What are they trying to hide?

ORIGIN AND HOME WORLD

The Draconians have visited Earth for millennia and are now believed to have made their home in the Draco constellation, on a rocky planet around the bright star Gamma Draconis or Etamin. This is around 148 light years from Earth. However, Draconian myth-legend is that Earth is one of their original homes and that a species of humanoid reptiles still lives deep within the planet.

The Draconians are an ancient race in the universe and certainly regard themselves as superior to many of the alien species they encounter. We know that they fought a great war against the Insectoids that spanned many galaxies. We're unaware of the current status of the Draconians and the Insectoids but they certainly won't be sending each other Christmas cards.

> **LITTLE IS KNOWN OF THEIR ACTUAL HOME WORLD. GREY INTELLIGENCE SUGGESTS THAT IT'S A DRY, BARREN, VOLCANIC WORLD, COVERED IN VAST STONE TEMPLES AND UNIVERSITIES, SOME OF WHICH ARE THOUSANDS OF YEARS OLD. IT'S SAID THAT THE DRACONIAN LIBRARIES CONTAIN NEARLY EVERY BOOK EVER PUBLISHED IN THE UNIVERSE, INCLUDING THE LOST WORKS OF HOMER, THE COMEDIES OF ARISTOTLE AND ALL JACKIE COLLINS'S BOOKS.**

MEN IN BLACK REPORT – AGENT MIB788 – LAGOS, NIGERIA

▶ A NOTE ON CONSPIRACIES

DRACONIAN CONSPIRACIES

The Draconians are experts at creating conspiracy theories and it has been estimated that over 53% of the alien sites on the internet are either directly run or funded by the Draconians to help spread confusion. This species delights in creating misinformation and chaos among humans and has been linked to everything from mock Grey abductions to kidnapping and cloning world leaders. They've also been closely tied to the New Age movement, seeing it as a chance to pacify humanity by stealth.

ISN'T EVERY FAMOUS PERSON A CLONE?

16/03 jb

THE MOON LANDING HAPPENED, RIGHT?

Almost 50% of the population now doubt that the moon landings of 1969 ever took place, but this is one conspiracy the Ministry of Alien Defence can clear up. On 20 July 1969, the Apollo 11 lunar module landed on Earth's moon. That's a fact. Were the aliens pleased about it? No way. In fact the Little Green Men were livid, believing that they'd already claimed the Moon for themselves. However, they did little more than lodge a formal complaint with the relevant authority before concentrating on their plans to take over the planet.

NEW LEVELS OF SNEAKINESS

Through the limited intelligence we have on the secretive Draconians, we know that they've been involved in virtually every field of espionage and deception on the planet. Their most recent areas of activity have included cyber-crime and in 2010 they were thought to have masterminded a major security breach of the US military's mainframe in which they slightly amended millions of fields of data, doing an estimated $500 million worth of damage.

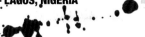

INSECTOIDS (THE HIVE, THE SPECIES)

Of all the species currently known to us, the Insectoids are perhaps the most 'alien' to humanity. We have no direct experience of these creatures and all the information we have has come to us via the Greys or captured Draconian clones. In fact we don't even know how the species refers to itself; the Greys refer to them simply as the 'Hive'.

The Insectoids are a highly xenophobic species who consider all other life forms to be akin to pollution. They migrate from one system or galaxy to another, with their home nests being made on great hollowed-out asteroids and planetoids. It isn't yet understood what motivates a migration of the colony but our best deduction is that the purpose is resource utilisation. In other words, the Insectoid hive moves into a system, strips it bare and then moves on to the next, eradicating any life forms within hundreds of light years.

ACCORDING TO THE GREYS, THE INSECTOIDS WILL NOT TOLERATE ANY ALIEN SPECIES WITHIN A SPECIFIC RANGE OF THEIR HOME WORLD OR NEST – WHICH IS WHERE THEIR RULING 'QUEEN' IS BASED. THEY AREN'T INTERESTED IN LEARNING ABOUT OTHER LIFE FORMS, EMPIRE BUILDING OR ALLIANCES – FOR THEM, ALL LIFE IS SEEN AS EXPENDABLE.

▶ APPEARANCE AND ABILITIES

WHAT WE KNOW!

Through eons of evolution, the Insectoids have developed what's known as a 'command bug' to coordinate their growing empire. Their Queen used to serve this purpose, but now these intelligent creatures can create and adapt orders 'on site' and according to the conditions.

An Insectoid is bipedal with a sizeable brain and its slim body is lightly armoured with bone. It can communicate either by emitting clicks or by releasing chemical elements. All soldier drones are equipped with tougher bone armour with a slimy coating that makes key areas of their bodies – such as the thorax – highly resistant to energy weapons.

HEIGHT	Unknown
WEIGHT	Unknown
COLOUR	Unknown
LIKES	Other Insectoids, their Queen and 1980s synth pop
DISLIKES	All other life forms, non-binary languages

PHYSICAL FEATURES

▶ It's unlikely that you'll encounter an Insectoid in any battle for Earth. The common element is their insect-like appearance such as a body or thorax and mandibles.

▶ Although referred to as the Insectoids, several of the variations currently known to us have a distinctly arachnid feel to them.

▶ All types of Insectoids have the same core elements, which include antennae (their primary communication and sensory organ), thorax (core of the body), compound eyes and mandibles (ranging from delicate scientific tweezers to those capable of cutting through steel).

Practise on the ants outside

ABILITIES

▶ We have no definite information on the speed and agility of Insectoids but alien biologists on Earth predict that their capabilities broadly match those of insects on Earth, so we can expect running speeds of up to 50mph.

▶ Importantly, no Insectoid variation feels any pain or emotion. The higher classes operate on detached logic, their decision-making unbiased by any emotional or compassionate response. Lower down the scale, worker drones will willingly sacrifice themselves to support the colony.

▶ The Insectoid species has the ability to create billions of additional life forms as required. Over millions of years they have perfected their reproductive process, which now takes place in humid tunnel-like caves and artificial caverns.

ALIEN KNOWLEDGE 101
THE INSECTOID AGENDA

This is one area we're very clear on – if an Insectoid ship moves into our solar system we can be sure that the plan will be to eradicate all life on Earth. By the time one of their larger hive ships enters, we can be 100% sure that humanity faces a battle for its very survival.

The Insectoids travel around different galaxies in an apparently random pattern, sometimes moving thousands of light years from their current home. They maintain some presence in their system of origin but don't seem to have a 'home world' in the sense that we understand. Rather, their home is wherever the Queen in based.

◀ COMMAND BUG

This is an artist's impression of an Insectoid command bug based on information supplied by the Greys during their interaction with humanity.

ALIEN MOTIVATION MATRIX: 5
EXTERMINATORS

The Insectoids aren't empire builders in the traditional sense but their presence in a system requires that all other life forms be eradicated. It's believed that they then go on to use all of the resources in the location before the hive continues on its inter-galactic migrations across the universe.

ALIEN TECHNOLOGY MATRIX: T6
UNIVERSE MOVERS

With the power-generation and propulsion technology to send ships across the universe, the Insectoids have developed far beyond humanity and even other advanced species such as the Greys. Little is known of Insectoid technology other than our belief that they possess a caste of brain creatures that can power their asteroids and planetoid hive ships far beyond the speed of light.

THE INSECTOID SPECIES IS XENOPHOBIC TO SUCH A DEGREE THAT ANY ALIEN INFLUENCE MUST BE ERADICATED. IT MAY BE THAT IN THE PAST THEIR CULTURE WAS MORE BALANCED AND OPEN, BUT NOW HUMANITY IS FACED WITH A TRULY FRIGHTENING OPPONENT.

An artist's impression of a common bug!

ALIEN KNOWLEDGE 101

SOCIETY

Any comparison with insect life forms on Earth is useful to a degree: for example, Insectoids still inhabit 'nests' and are centrally governed by a Queen. They've also evolved specialised creatures such as soldiers and workers, as with ant colonies on Earth. However, it must be remembered that their hive is thousands of years ahead in terms of evolution.

The Insectoids have had powered space flight for eons and their T6 listing on the Alien Technology Matrix means that they're capable of travelling across the known universe and generating the massive amounts of energy required. It's important, therefore, not to assume that their ant-like social structure is a low-technology civilisation. The level of specialism in the hive has seen the development not only of soldiers and workers but also a builder drone, command bug and a large jelly-type mass known by the Greys as a mind bug.

ORIGIN AND HOME WORLD

The Insectoids are believed to have originated in the NGC 7378 galaxy in the Aquarius constellation. It's thought that their species is one of the oldest life forms in the universe and that its adaptability has made it one of the most successful. The planet T-78388-7378 is identified as the home world of the Insectoids by the Greys but even they have never visited this quadrant of space.

Insects became the dominant species on T-78388-7378 and over several million years developed the social structure, language and technology to expand into their immediate space. According to legend, the Insectoids were originally a peaceful species, content to ignore aliens unless they directly threatened the hive. However, it's believed that a devastating early war with a now long-forgotten alien species warped the governing psychology of the Insectoids such that they cannot now tolerant any alien life form. The planet T-78388-7378 itself is believed to have been sterilised of any life.

THE INSECTOIDS ARE EXPERTS IN GENETIC MANIPULATION AND CAN QUICKLY ADAPT THEIR CORE MODELS, PARTICULARLY THE SOLDIERS, TO MEET THE CHALLENGE OF A PARTICULAR OPPONENT OR ENVIRONMENT. THIS IS THE REAL STRENGTH OF THE HIVE. AN OPPONENT MIGHT DESTROY BILLIONS OF SOLDIERS USING A NEW WEAPON BUT THE INSECTOIDS WILL SIMPLY DEVELOP A VARIANT THAT CAN COMBAT THE WEAPON OR IS RESISTANT TO IT.

INSECTOID TYPES

The Insectoid species has taken specialism to an extreme – developing hundreds of different castes to undertake the myriad tasks involved in sustaining a hive of billions of creatures. This section outlines the key types currently known and most likely to be encountered during any invasion of Earth. There are doubtless others that are unknown outside Insectoid space. Both the Greys and the Draconians maintain an immense buffer zone between their space and that of the Insectoids.

> **"INSECTS ARE THE GREAT SUCCESS STORY OF LIFE ON EARTH IN EVERY MEASURE SO IT'S NOT A SURPRISE THAT THEY HAVE EVOLVED AS THE PRIME SPECIES ON OTHER WORLDS."**
> **DR SOO JAN-LEE, EXTRA-TERRESTRIAL ENTOMOLOGIST**

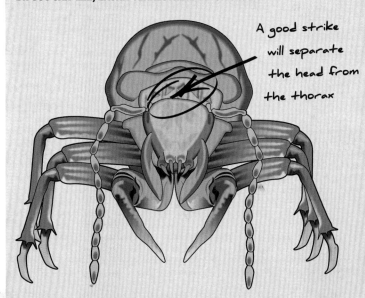

A good strike will separate the head from the thorax

▲ WORKER DRONES
CLASSICS, HIVE BUGS

Colourless and transparent, worker drones are designed for general labour, tunnelling and carrying. They're blind and move by using their two long antennae. These creatures are basically defenceless: although they can bite with their mandibles, drones lack th intelligence to do anything other than follow orders. It's estimated that around 70% of an Insectoid colony is made up of worker drones. They're expendable and work in vast swarms.

▶ SOLDIER DRONES
FIGHTERS, WARRIOR BUGS

These terrifying armoured Insectoids are the mainstay of the attack swarm. Armed with various configurations of stings, jaws and pointed legs, these creatures are fearless killers that will attempt to destroy any opponent regardless of the cost to themselves. Most operate on six legs and can be adapted to carry weapons such as poison bombs or acid sprays.

How does it fire these jets of acid?

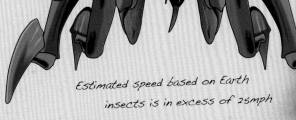

Estimated speed based on Earth insects is in excess of 25mph

◀ SCIENCE BUGS
INVENTORS, 2.0 BUGS

The armour-less science bug is only found inside the main hive or an asteroid ship. They have eight eyes and a detachable brain stem that enables them to be relocated on to a different body if required. This has enabled these specialist workers to develop their science and engineering skills. They have a set of delicate mandibles specially designed for detailed work. The body is translucent, with a clear black string running through the centre of it.

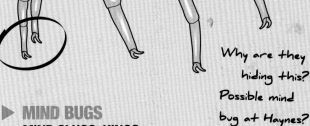

Why are they hiding this? Possible mind bug at Haynes?

▶ MIND BUGS
MIND SLUGS, KINGS

Not even the Greys have seen an Insectoid mind bug. It's believed that these vast, sprawling creatures exist only inside asteroid ships and are fed by slave drones. These Insectoids are said to be the collective intelligence of the Insectoid species, operating almost as computer servers, storing knowledge and experience on individual creatures. It's thought that each Insectoid hive ship has only one such bug and therefore it would be an obvious target for any attack.

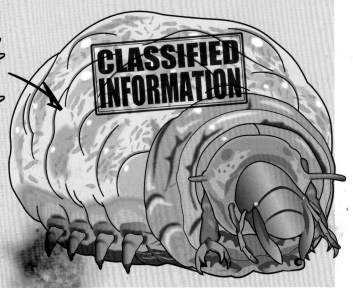

CLASSIFIED INFORMATION

OIOIIOOI OIIOIIII OIIIOIOI OOIOOOOO OIIOOOOI OIIIOOIO OIIOOIOI OOIOOOOO OIIOOOOI OOIOOOOO
OIIOOOII OIIOIIOO OIIOOIOI OIIIOIIO OIIOOIOI OIIIOOIO OOIOOOOO OIIOOOII OIIOIIOO OIIOIIII OIIIOOIII OIIIOOII

33

⚙ TECHNOLOGY

The Insectoid species uses hollow asteroids as inter-stellar 'hive ships'. As a hive ship has never been seen in our solar system, this schematic is based on Little Green Men records, which are sparse. Each hive ship can carry an estimated 1–2 billion drones. Hive ships are typically sent to a system to cleanse it of all 'alien life' before a larger planetary ship arrives with the rest of the colony. Although considered one of the oldest species in the universe, the Insectoids favour a balance of technology and biology to meet their objectives.

Pods are designed for a one-way trip – to land the soldiers on a planet's surface

What's their speed?

OBSERVATION DOME

It's unlikely that the Insectoids use this area to enjoy views of the star-filled universe. Our current hypothesis is that it's some kind of galactic greenhouse – possibly to support the growing of the mould and fungus that's their primary food source.

1. Asteroid with limited water but elements such as nickel, cobalt and rhodium.
2. Forward shield generators designed to protect the hive colony in deep space.
3. Drone launchers – when a hive ship enters a system, thousands of bio-mechanical drones are fired into space and at any nearby planets; it's these probes that alert the hive to the presence of life.
4. Glutinous mass – believed to be the ship's brain.

5. Drone launching pods – these small rock vessels are unpowered and fired towards their target.
6. Drone launching pod – typically has six drone warriors.
7. Breeding chambers – damp, moist caverns, covered with rotting fungus.
8. Maggot drones hatching.
9. Armoury – designed to create weapons for individual Insectoid creatures, particularly the soldiers.

10. Bio-engineering – much Insectoid technology is grown rather than built.
11. Ship's core.
12. Command centre.
13. Fungal cavern (food store).
14. Observation dome.
15. Crystallised binary records chamber – each Insectoid hive ship seems to carry the entirety of Insectoid knowledge.
16. Propulsion system unknown – hyper-space capability estimated.

▶ THE SCIENCE OF BUGS

A SPECIAL REPORT BY SOO-JAN LEE

Any study of the Insectoid species can by definition only be theoretical as we've never seen any examples of the species and are reliant completely on intelligence from untrustworthy former allies. I should also emphasise that I have some reservations about the Insectoid outlines provided in this section – particularly the Insectoid brain – as they seem to have little substance in reality.

Firstly, let's be clear. We already live on an insect planet. There are over 900,000 different types of living insect in the world and they account for almost 90% of all the species on Earth. Our current estimate is that some 10 quintillion individual insects are alive at any one time. Relative to their size, insects are the strongest, fastest and most poisonous life forms on Earth, and they have the most developed societies.

It's no surprise, therefore, that elsewhere in the universe insect life has developed instead of, for example, mammals or reptiles. One study has estimated that over 80% of the billions of species within the known universe are likely to be Insectoid in origin.

DEALING WITH INSECTOID ALIENS

▶ Insects don't think and feel the same way as other species. Their brains work completely differently and we have no reason to believe that this would change as the species advances.

▶ Insect races have probably developed specialised insect types to help them organise themselves efficiently. They'll be ruthless in their decision-making, thinking nothing of sacrificing billions of drones to protect the colony.

▶ Targeting the Queen would be a misguided tactic as there are frequently billions of female drones that can easily be developed into a new Queen. In addition, the Queen is likely to be at the centre of the hive and therefore well protected.

INSECTS ARE THE GREAT ADAPTERS OF THE UNIVERSE AND THEORETICAL PROJECTIONS HINT THAT AT SOME POINT THE ENTIRE UNIVERSE WILL BECOME INSECTOID. IT'S POSSIBLE THAT SOME DIMENSIONS ARE ALREADY DOMINATED BY A SINGLE INSECTOID SPECIES THAT HAS ERADICATED ALL OTHER FORMS OF LIFE.

ALIEN KNOWLEDGE 101
ALIEN DISTRIBUTION

According to the mathematical modelling of Dr Soo Jan-Lee and her team, the universe is already Insectoid. The figures given here have been taken from an article entitled 'The End of Carbon Chauvinism', which was published in *The American Journal of Astrobiology*, VXII, pages 920–922.

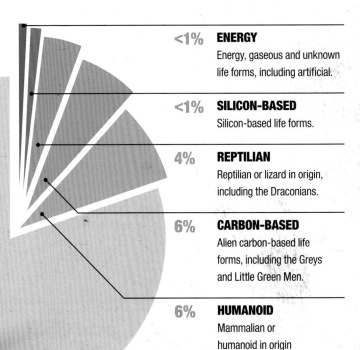

<1% ENERGY
Energy, gaseous and unknown life forms, including artificial.

<1% SILICON-BASED
Silicon-based life forms.

4% REPTILIAN
Reptilian or lizard in origin, including the Draconians.

6% CARBON-BASED
Alien carbon-based life forms, including the Greys and Little Green Men.

6% HUMANOID
Mammalian or humanoid in origin (not all oxygen-breathing).

80% INSECTOID
Insectoid in origin, including arachnid and derived life forms.

NORDIC (MIRROR MAN, GLIMMER MAN)

The Nordics are a highly advanced species of inter-dimensional travellers who have visited Earth many times over the centuries. They can appear in different forms but most commonly they're seen as glowing, platinum-blond humanoids – hence the term 'Nordic'.

In some ways we know a great deal about the Nordics. We know that they travel throughout the universe, that they're opposed to violence of any kind, and that they have a keen interest in philosophy. In other ways we know very little. We don't know where they come from and we know nothing of the technology they use or why they've been coming to Earth for so many years.

The Nordics have never hidden their agenda; they just don't speak of it and refuse to be drawn in by human questioning. It's hard to tell exactly how many dimensional beings have visited our planet but there's certainly evidence of them throughout history. For example, the Anglo-Saxon Chronicles tell of a 'light man' who appeared to King Harold in AD 1053.

ACCORDING TO THE NORDICS, THEY'RE PART OF A GROUP OF INTER-DIMENSIONAL SPECIES THAT HAVE ASCENDED FROM THE CURRENT UNIVERSE AND WHO NOW TRAVEL 'EXISTENCE' GATHERING WISDOM AND KNOWLEDGE.

APPEARANCE AND ABILITIES

WHAT WE KNOW!

Throughout history the Nordics have been known by many names, such as 'Mirror Men' or 'Glimmer People'. They're humanoid in appearance but are said to have a distinct unearthly glow about them. Nordics have come in many forms over the years but seem to prefer the tall, fair, corporeal form that gives rise to their name.

Nordics seem unable to grasp some of the very real challenges we face on Earth, such as how to defend our planet. It may be that they've evolved so far that they're now unable to comprehend the vulnerability of less-developed creatures such as ourselves.

You really are perfect aren't you?

HEIGHT	2 metres
WEIGHT	Just right
COLOUR	Glowing bronze
LIKES	Long, hypothetical conversations, Peter Gabriel's music
DISLIKES	Aggression, violence and direct questions

PHYSICAL FEATURES

▶ Build is humanoid and muscular. Witnesses have encountered both male and female Nordics and it seems that the Nordics can adapt their form to ensure that humans are most comfortable in their presence.

▶ Their skin is a glowing bronze; some observers have referred to it as an 'inhuman glow', free of blemishes.

▶ The Nordics appear to be ageless, supporting the theory that they appear in this form to present themselves more reassuringly to humanity.

▶ ██████████████████████████

and with the apparent absence of any veins.

ABILITIES

▶ Nordics have a faint glow around them, perhaps due to the inter-dimensional nature of their travel. We suspect this to be residual energy from their dematerialisation process.

▶ Nordics move slowly and deliberately. They can freely communicate in most languages of the world but are also adept at telepathy. They'll only enter a human's mind when the human has agreed to such a link.

▶ In their corporeal form, Nordics have similar strength and tolerances as a normal human, although they don't seem to feel cold or heat.

▶ Nordics can disappear or 'evaporate' at will. A brief shining light appears behind them and they're gone.

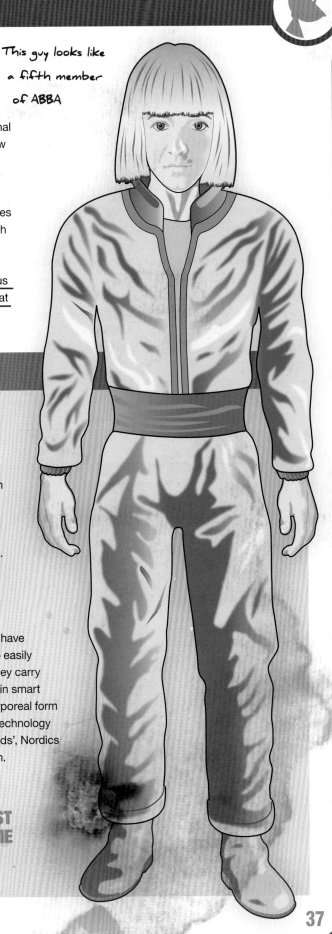

ALIEN KNOWLEDGE 101
THE NORDIC AGENDA

This guy looks like a fifth member of ABBA

According to the Nordics, they're part of a group of inter-dimensional species that have ascended from the current universe and who now travel 'existence' gathering wisdom and knowledge. It's hard to tell exactly how many so-called dimensional beings have visited our planet but there's certainly evidence for them throughout history. The Nordics are thought to be energy-beings who travel all universes searching for enlightenment. Needless to say, they don't get on with the Little Green Men. Their sharing comes not from offering their technology to humanity but their guidance and moral compass.

One fear is that they're judging humanity and that if they deem us unworthy they could, with their immense power, not only ensure that we cease to exist but also that we never existed in the first place.

2/08
lm

ALIEN MOTIVATION MATRIX: 1
OBSERVERS

Despite having god-like powers, the Nordics and other inter-dimensional light beings have never threatened or shown any interest in invading our planet. Their interest seems focused on the developing philosophies of humanity. They're unwilling to get involved in human affairs and avoid answering any questions that they deem unnecessary for human evolution. We believe that they know what will happen in the future but refuse to give us any clues.

ALIEN TECHNOLOGY MATRIX: T7
GOD-LIKE *'God Complex'*

Dimensional travel requires vast amounts of energy and as yet we have no idea how the Nordics generate this power or how they move so easily between dimensions. When they manifest themselves on Earth, they carry no technological equipment or special clothing. They may appear in smart clothes or rags. But these are no illusions as they do appear in corporeal form and have been known to share meals with humans. Their level of technology is millions of years beyond our understanding. If referred to as 'Gods', Nordics become visibly uncomfortable and are quick to deny this assertion.

WE'RE THE SAME AS PLANTS, AS TREES, AS HUMANS, AS THE RAIN THAT FALLS. WE CONSIST OF THAT WHICH IS AROUND US, WE'RE THE SAME AS EVERYTHING. IF WE DESTROY SOMETHING AROUND US, WE DESTROY OURSELVES.

TECHNOLOGY

The Nordics don't arrive on Earth in 'ships' as we understand them. They appear via energy portal that they seem to be able to create at will. They carry no energy source and our theoretical understanding indicates that opening such a portal would require the energy of a small sun to complete. The Nordic species has clearly evolved beyond physical technology and somehow manages to harness the latent energy that's present everywhere in the universe. They carry no weapons or communication devices, although they seem to enjoy all forms of pocket watches and are fascinated by the clocks we have created on Earth.

Advances in our own knowledge of string theory and the quantum mechanics of the universe should bring us closer to understanding how Nordic technology functions, but as much of it's millions of years ahead of our own we're unlikely to grasp anything significant in the next few decades. The Nordics aren't a species we can rely on to share technology that could save Earth or help us to fight an alien invasion.

SOCIETY

Inter-dimensional hypothesis not covered in my GCSE Physics course work – what are they hiding?

We imagine Nordic society to be like a perfect hippie colony of the future – where arguments, aggression and violence have been consigned to the history books. Nordics have been visitors to Earth throughout our recorded history and have always been patient and non-violent. They appear to have reached a pinnacle of 'Zen' such that nothing can upset their balance. They appreciate philosophy, particularly Buddhism, to which they have a great affinity. They appear incapable of understanding humanity's penchant for violence and sometimes seem frustrated, even upset, by it.

> **THEIR RESPONSES TO QUESTIONS CAN BE OBTUSE AND INDIRECT, LEAVING THE HUMAN QUESTIONER UNSURE AS TO WHETHER THEIR QUESTION WAS ANSWERED OR NOT. THEY OFTEN REFER TO HUMANITY BEING 'TESTED' AND ONLY RELUCTANTLY REVEAL INFORMATION ABOUT OTHER SPECIES IN THE UNIVERSE.**
>
> **MEN IN BLACK REPORT (AGENT MIB 997), LHASA, TIBET**

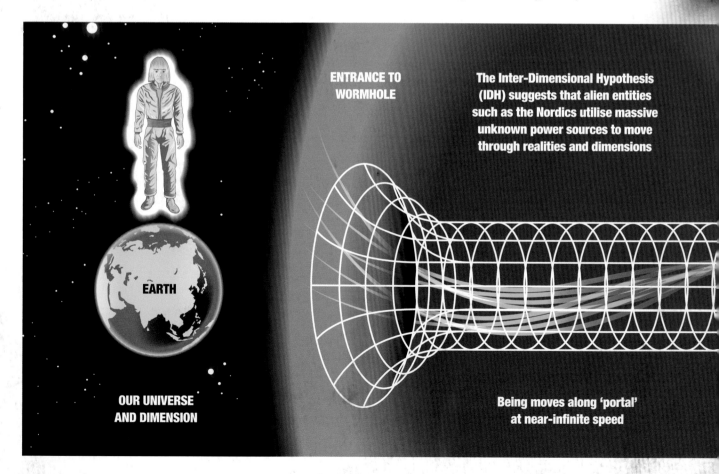

ENTRANCE TO WORMHOLE

The Inter-Dimensional Hypothesis (IDH) suggests that alien entities such as the Nordics utilise massive unknown power sources to move through realities and dimensions

EARTH

OUR UNIVERSE AND DIMENSION

Being moves along 'portal' at near-infinite speed

> **THEY MOVE ACROSS DIMENSIONS AND DO NOT REGARD SPACE OR TIME IN THE SAME WAY WE DO. IT COULD BE THAT THEY EXIST ONLY IN ENERGY FORM AND SO CAN EXIST EVERYWHERE AT THE SAME TIME.**
> **DR JANE SORENSEN, HELSINKI INSTITUTE OF THEORETICAL SCIENCE**

ORIGIN AND HOME WORLD

Despite their human appearance, it's believed that the Nordics aren't revealing themselves in their real form. The only information ever released about their origin was to Tibetan monks. According to the monks, the Nordics inhabit what modern science refers to as the 10th Dimensional Reality – the sum of all universes and their outcomes.

One current line of investigation theorises that the Nordics may in fact be humans from millions of years in the future who have perhaps returned to support our development. To date, the Nordics have resisted any attempts to have them share their knowledge of space travel with us and they won't be drawn into any discussion about whether they would support humanity if Earth were to be invaded.

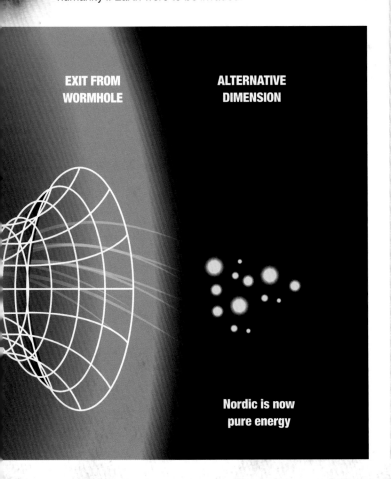

EXIT FROM
WORMHOLE

ALTERNATIVE
DIMENSION

Nordic is now
pure energy

▶ SPECIAL CONTACT PROTOCOLS

MATERIALISATION

History has shown that Nordics appear first as an apparition – often confused in the past as a 'ghost'. This is merely the first stage of their materialisation in this dimension. If they deem further exploration worthy, they typically follow up with a visit, appearing in the same location and slowly taking on a corporeal form.

A NON-VIOLENT FIRST RESPONSE

Don't try to hurl anything at the apparition. Never, ever attack a Nordic or other 'light being' in its corporeal form. Don't wait for it to appear then think you're doing humanity a favour by trying to steal its 'secrets'. You won't harm it and, at best, the being will disappear and possibly never return. At worst, the inter-dimensional species may view us as unworthy of continued existence due to chronic violence, and destroy us all without us even knowing it.

BE PATIENT AND RESPECTFUL

As the being materialises from another dimension, wait patiently and then bow respectfully, but not in worship. Smile and hold up the palm of your hand in the universal sign of greeting.

SOME BACKGROUND MUSIC

Play suitable New Age music or some Stevie Nicks in the background. Conversation topics for Nordics include the joy of life and Zen philosophy or any Fleetwood Mac album apart from 'Tusk'. Ensure that the 'aura' is kept calm and tranquil – these beings haven't expended the energy of our sun in crossing dimensions just to hear you say, 'OMG, this is so totes amaze!'

CONSIDER YOUR RESPONSE CAREFULLY AND SPEAK SLOWLY AND CLEARLY – THE BEINGS MAY BE ASSESSING YOU AND YOUR INTELLECT. IF YOU ANSWER ANY QUESTION INCORRECTLY, NORDICS WILL OFTEN SAY TO YOU 'THIS IS NOT CORRECT' – TO WHICH YOU SHOULD RESPOND, SOMEWHAT MYSTERIOUSLY 'OR IS IT?', HINTING AT SOME DEEPER MEANING. ONLY USE THIS IF YOU REALLY HAVE TO 'WING IT'.

A HISTORY OF ALIEN CONTACT

Humanity has been troubled by the alien menace for many thousands of years. This section looks at our experience with alien contact over the course of history, including a range of scenarios from UFO sightings to abductions, implants and even attempted invasions.

To date, alien intervention has been largely ignored by the academic community and as such there has never been a comprehensive history of extra-terrestrial activity on Earth. With our knowledge still fragmentary and large areas of study remaining unaddressed, the best we can do is to review some of the best-known incidents, those that dedicated experts and often amateurs have painstakingly researched for us.

ALIEN INTERVENTION HISTORIANS TEND TO DIVIDE THEIR SUBJECT INTO THREE MAIN SECTIONS THAT REVOLVE AROUND THE KEY EVENTS IN HUMAN/ALIEN RELATIONS – THE ROSWELL, NEW MEXICO CRASH OF 1947. MAYBE IN TIME THESE SECTIONS WILL BE FURTHER SUB-DIVIDED – BUT REMEMBER THAT ALIEN HISTORY IS A NEW SUBJECT AND IT IS HOPED THAT FURTHER RESEARCH WILL ADD TO OUR KNOWLEDGE IN THE DECADES AHEAD.

▶ PRE-HISTORY (UP TO 1939)

This era covers mainly pre-Roswell events and includes hundreds of mostly poorly documented and fragmentary accounts of contact, abduction and even attempted invasion right the way back to the dawn of man. Most of the case studies are reported only in part and some now feel more like legends and myths than verifiable history. However, these stories still have much to teach us. They prove that aliens have visited our planet for thousands of years if not more. And even these incomplete accounts suggest that the rate of intervention is increasing.

▶ MODERN (1939–80)

This period covers the spate of UFO appearances during and after World War Two, leading up to the Treaty of Greada in 1954, then up to the closure of the Dulce Airbase and the eviction of the Greys from the United States in 1980. These years represent a major shift in our relationship with aliens. After the Greys established a base on Earth under American sanction, it really did seem like Earth was 'open for business'. Unfortunately, the world isn't yet united enough to share knowledge of this encounter and the price of cooperation with the Greys is too high.

POST-ROSWELL (1980 ONWARDS)

This era begins in the bloody aftermath of the Dulce Airbase battle and is characterised by an ongoing and covert war against several potential alien invaders. The Greys, the Little Green Men and the Draconians all seem to be increasing their activity. But humanity is far from helpless and this period has seen the creation of the United Nations Office for Earth Defence in 2000 and major reforms in the Men in Black units.

Must separate fact from fiction... aliens real... Roswell real... Superman made up...

WE ARE NOT ALONE, WE HAVE NEVER BEEN ALONE!

MINISTRY OF ALIEN DEFENCE

THE PHARAOH ERASED FROM HISTORY

Any visitor to Egypt will quickly notice that in certain temples one particular cartouche has consistently been removed. Typically, it appears that some vandal has taken a chisel to the symbol and scarred the stone such that it's quite impossible to read the inscription. However, this isn't recent damage and radio-carbon dating has shown that most of the cartouches of the heretic Pharaoh Akhenaten were defaced shortly after his death in around 1330 BC.

THE LEGEND OF AKHENATEN

Akhenaten was lost from history until discoveries in the 19th century gradually enabled archeologists and ancient historians to piece together his story. His great crime – and the one reason why his name was removed from history – was his attempt to transfer the religious allegiance of the priest class and peasants from their pantheon of gods to just one god, called Aten (or Ra).

What brought this story to the attention of alien invasion experts is the fact that, in the few pictures that remain, Akhenaten and his wife Nefertiti are represented as having elongated heads and long, thin arms – which implies that

they may have been human/alien clones. This evidence alone wouldn't be sufficient as images of rulers were often stylised in the ancient world, but further indications of an extra-terrestrial link are offered by stone carvings that show the Pharaoh and his wife in 'communion' with a bright light from the sky. Could it be that the Pharaoh is taking orders from a creature he believes to be Aten?

It's fortunate that a cache of diplomatic correspondence known as the Amarna Letters has been unearthed and we have gained valuable insight into what was happening during this period of Egyptian history. In one communication to the King of Babylon, Akhenaten writes: 'We are overjoyed at news of the war against the Hittites. Great Aten has told me that we must grow our empire. He speaks to me in my mind and when I am taken inside his place of silver.' *4/03 mh*

The historical record about Akhenaten is frustratingly sparse but the evidence certainly points to an experiment in hybridisation. Unusually, Akhenaten's body has never been found. Some believe that it was burned by an angry priest class after his death – an action unheard of in ancient Egypt as it would have prevented him moving on to the next world.

If the legend of Akhenaten was a conspiracy, possibly by the Greys, to use religion to control humanity, it backfired upon Akhenaten's death; riots swept Egypt and the old order of gods was quickly restored. The aliens would have learned that using religion to control humanity is a delicate matter.

A HISTORY OF ALIEN CONTACT

PRE-HISTORY (UP TO 1939)

Our understanding of alien intervention during this period is very limited, with the most up-to-date and well-documented accounts, not surprisingly, being the most recent ones. From the classical world, we rely largely on second-hand accounts and fragmentary texts, very few of which can be corroborated by other sources.

Perhaps the most famous biblical reference to an alien encounter is found in the Book of Ezekiel, which in its opening chapter provides a notably authentic description of the landing of an uncloaked alien pod ship.

'And I looked, and, behold, a whirlwind came out of the north, a great cloud, and a fire infolding itself, and a brightness was about it, and out of the midst thereof as the colour of amber, out of the midst of the fire.' As the text goes on to suggest there were alien reptiles that quickly shape-shifted into human form such that they had 'the likeness of a man', this account would seem to describe the forced landing of a Draconian ship.

▶ THE NEPHILIM

One area demanding more academic attention and research are the Grey hybrid experiments that were known as the Nephilim in ancient times and are best recorded in the ancient book of Enoch.

> NOW IT CAME ABOUT, WHEN MEN BEGAN TO MULTIPLY ON THE FACE OF THE LAND, AND DAUGHTERS WERE BORN TO THEM, THAT THE SONS OF GOD SAW THAT THE DAUGHTERS OF MEN WERE BEAUTIFUL; AND THEY TOOK WIVES FOR THEMSELVES, WHOMEVER THEY CHOSE. THEN THE LORD SAID, 'MY SPIRIT SHALL NOT STRIVE WITH MAN FOREVER, BECAUSE HE ALSO IS FLESH; NEVERTHELESS HIS DAYS SHALL BE ONE HUNDRED AND TWENTY YEARS.' THE NEPHILIM WERE ON THE EARTH IN THOSE DAYS, AND ALSO AFTERWARD, WHEN THE SONS OF GOD CAME IN TO THE DAUGHTERS OF MEN, AND THEY BORE CHILDREN TO THEM. THOSE WERE THE MIGHTY MEN WHO WERE OF OLD, MEN OF RENOWN.
>
> GENESIS 6:1–4

It's thought that the Nephilim were wiped out by the Great Flood. Could they have been a first, tentative step on the part of the Greys to solve their reproductive challenges by DNA engineering? Perhaps we'll never know, as even the information provided by the Greys is sparse about this chapter of their history.

▶ THE HALF-LIZARD GREEK

Cecrops was a mythical king of the Greek city-state of Athens, most famous for two main things.

Firstly, he's frequently represented as being 'a face with a tail'. He was said to have been half-man, half-serpent, which immediately suggests a shape-shifting Draconian. Art historians have suggested that many of the images we have of him were created many centuries after his death and have most probably been idealised, as often happens with mythical figures. However, the contemporary evidence we have suggests a lizard-man in the top spot as one of the first kings of Athens.

Secondly, it's believed that Cecrops introduced a radical 'breeding' programme to high society in Athens by creating the concept of marriage among the promiscuous nobility.

Cecrops became a powerful ruler and left a dynasty in his wake that ruled for five generations. However, it's his intervention in the coupling of Athenian big-wigs that seems to have been his biggest legacy for subsequent generations.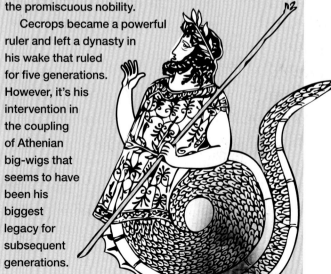

THE FOUR DRAGON KINGS

Historians of Chinese civilisation have always taken the legend of the Dragon King as religious myth-tale but emerging evidence about Draconian designs on Earth has cast a different light on this segment of history. The fact that whole kingdoms were said to be ruled by 'shape-shifting lizards' was enough to make even the most sceptical historian sit up and take note. There are also countless reams of imperial documentation from the era to back up the hundreds of pieces of artwork and pottery showing the Dragon Kings.

In classical Chinese mythology there are four Dragon Kings, each of which rules one of the Four Seas surrounding the Celestial Kingdom. In this interpretation Lake Baikal is included as the Sea of the North. These unusual kings are said to have ruled large tracts of land around 300–200 BC and to have performed miracles such as flying and firing heat over vast distances – and, of course, changing shape.

We know little about these rulers other than what has been written about them in classic novels such as *Fengshen Bang* and *Journey to the West*, but they've been featured in Chinese folklore for hundreds if not thousands of years. The four kings – Ao Ch'in, Ao Jun, Ao Kuang and Ao Shun – are said to have ruled from the seas, extending their control over any coastal towns and villages. The Dragon Kings were guarded by their own soldiers and, according to legend, they lived in underwater 'crystal palaces' that could fly. Needless to say, their power is thought to have been unrivaled by any other warlords.

A ROMAN ENCOUNTER

In AD 150 a Roman nobleman named Hermas, brother of Pope Pius, had an extra-terrestrial experience on the road between Capua and Rome. His account was recorded in *The Vision of Hermas*, an early Christian work from which the following quote is taken.

'I saw a beast like a piece of pottery about 100 feet in size, multi-coloured on top and shooting fiery rays; it landed in a dust cloud. From a great pot walked a two-legged serpent, as tall as man most mighty. He was accompanied by a maiden clad in white. He spoke with her before she left the pot. The serpent saw me and, for a time, I was drawn to his gaze. I rushed forward and drew my dagger, ready to grapple with this demon made flesh while my servants fled in fear. Then, in the haze of midday, the great pot boiled away and vanished.'

A recently discovered document, however, suggests that Hermas may not have been entirely truthful in his version of events. A slave who later became a free man gave a somewhat different account.

'Hermas ran faster than any of us servants. He even pushed one of the grey-haired water carriers over to aid his flight. He was howling and screaming like the wind and would not stop shouting "Big Snake!" until hours after the pot had vanished like the mist.'

A HISTORY OF ALIEN CONTACT

THE MODERN ERA (1939–80)

Many experts believe that it was the use of the first jet propulsion aircraft and the exploding of the two nuclear bombs over Japan during World War Two that directly led to the massive increase in UFO sightings and abduction reports during the 1940s and 1950s. Indeed, it's no coincidence that this era also brought one of the classic science-fiction movies and almost hysterical levels of panic about 'little green men' or 'invaders from Mars'. Of course, there's some truth behind the science fiction, with aliens such as the Greys and what we now term the Little Green Men beginning to take humanity much more seriously, even seeing us a potential threat.

THE MODERN ERA IN THE HISTORY OF ALIENS ON EARTH IS DOMINATED BY THE EVENTS SURROUNDING THE ROSWELL CRASH. THIS INCIDENT EVENTUALLY LEADS TO HUMANITY'S FIRST FORMAL CONTACT WITH AN ALIEN RACE.

THE ROSWELL CRASH

No single alien event on Earth has generated so much debate, myth and web chatter than the crash of a single Grey saucer in the New Mexico desert in 1947. It's important to note that this wasn't the first UFO crash on Earth but the timing couldn't have been more significant. America was in the grips of anti-communist paranoia, with enemies being seen behind every rock. Yet America was still essentially a free society with a powerful independent press, growing broadcast media and some great pioneers in live journalism. It was into this fertile soil that a stray Grey saucer came down and was recovered by the US military. And, what's more, there were survivors on board.

▶ The crash of a Type 1 Grey saucer near Roswell is the most significant alien encounter of modern times, producing hundreds of witnesses and much photographic evidence. It received significant media coverage at the time before being clumsily covered up by the US government.

▶ LITTLE GREEN MEN AND THE NAZIS

Exactly what did US Air Force pilot Colonel Benjamin R. Ryker shoot down during a raid over Germany in January 1945? Well, there are several amazing facts about the Colonel, who survived the war and went on to own a popular fast-food chain in America. Firstly, he was a prominent member of 332nd Fighter Group, which is more popularly known as the 'Tuskegee Airmen' – a group of African-American pilots who took to the skies over Europe from 1943 onwards, battling the Nazis and discrimination as they went. Secondly, and perhaps more importantly, he seems to be the only human pilot to have shot down a black triangle ship!

'We left the big birds to continue their flight home while I and a couple of other red tips [nickname for their North American P-51 Mustangs, which had unique red markings on the tail] broke off to fly over the nearby Warhearn Airbase, which we knew had been active. As I was completing my first pass, a black object flew past me at incredible speed. I banked right and lost eyeball contact with the target. I regained visual contact and noticed its

- The Grey saucer that came down contained a number of bodies and at least one alien that was still alive.
- In later contact with the Greys, we learned that the crash was most likely caused by a junior member of the crew flying the craft under the influence of an exotic substance known as 'gleek', with apparently has a mild hallucinogenic effect on the delicate biology of the Greys.
- The alien survivors were taken to Groom Lake Airbase in Nevada. This later became a centre of alien research and is known by the scientists who work there as Area 51 or 'Dreamland' – the nickname arose because of the technological advances that were made there as they debriefed the captured Greys and examined the saucer.

Luftwaffe markings. For a few seconds I thought it was one of the foo fighters all the guys had been talking about.

'By now, I was alone over the base with a single anti-aircraft gun opening up. Their shots were so off target I suspected they were conscripted Poles missing on purpose, so I had a clear run. I flew a wide arc then came back in behind the black ship, which was now landing. It was a black triangle with markings on it. I'd never seen an aircraft like it but it was marked so it was game. I gave it a five-second blast of cannon and must have hit it because a plume of grey smoke shot into the air. With the heat off from any ground fire, I made another pass and saw the ship was now leaning to one side and seemed to be ablaze. I noticed a Nazi pilot dashing away but I didn't have enough ammunition for a second salvo. But what happened next took my breath away.

'First, I saw a small figure in a white suit climb out and run away from the wreck. It was wearing a much larger space helmet and can't have been more than a few feet tall. The next few seconds were something I'll never forget. The black triangle craft looked like it was just about to blow but instead there was a strange haze above it and then it disappeared into thin air. It's like the whole wreckage rose up and imploded.'

FOO FIGHTERS

During World War Two there were reports from pilots on both sides about their planes being 'buzzed' by fast-flying groups of lights or 'foo fighters' as they were known at the time. Early German experiments with jet propulsion such as the Messerschmitt Me262 seemed to be particularly vulnerable to alien interest. It's now believed that these lights were automatic alien probes that had perhaps been alerted by the new speeds being achieved by these aircraft.

However, the craft Colonel Ryker destroyed on the runway was no probe. For starters, it appears to have been crewed by a German pilot and a small alien figure. Rumours of alien connections to the Nazis have persisted for many decades but for the most part with very little documentary or first-hand evidence.

EVIDENCE OF A PACT BETWEEN THE NAZIS AND THE LITTLE GREEN MEN IS HARD TO PIN DOWN. NO HYBRID ALIEN SHIPS WERE FOUND AFTER THE WAR AND IT SEEMS LIKELY THAT THE VISITORS HEADED FOR THE STARS AS THE NAZI REGIME BEGAN TO COLLAPSE.

AREA 51 (DREAMLAND)

Groom Lake – more commonly known as Area 51 – is one of the world's centres of knowledge on all things extra-terrestrial. It's attached to Edwards Air Force Base in Nevada. Area 51 covers some 80 square miles of the most closely guarded space on Earth and for many years has been the home of the American response to the alien threat. The US Air Force still maintains a media black-out on the base many scientists refer to as 'Dreamland' and most aerial images online have been doctored.

▶ MAP OF AREA 51

1. Perimeter extending some 10 miles – exclusion zone and armed patrols.
2. 'Dream Road' – slang for the main route through the base.
3. Alien compound (now thought to be unused).
4. Bio-dome, constructed in 1982 (appears on very few photographs).
5. S5 – alien intelligence and debriefing centre.
6. S4 – part of the reverse-engineering block.
7. S3 – formerly a 'Men in Black' building, now used by the UN.
8. Hangar 1 – known as the 'Magic Box', this houses two crashed grey saucers, both Type 1s; the first is from Roswell, the origin of the other is unknown.
9. Hangar 2 – where alien technology is built into new human-made aircraft, such as the 'stealth' designs that originated in the 1980s.
10. Bio-Science Block and ET morgue – a copy of the 1986 inventory logs seven Grey bodies in various conditions and two Little Green Men.
11. Data Block – a small complex of servers and systems analysing alien data and technology.
12. S10 – a language block, where translations are completed.
13. The 'Kill Zone' – where trespassers will be stopped, with the use of lethal force.
14. The 'Gallery' – a huge concrete hangar used for testing of energy weapons.
15. Accommodation and guard blocks for those working on site – some 1,000 people.
16. The 'UN Building' – a bomb-proof bunker facility so named because it's where the Treaty of Greada was signed.
17. The 'Green House' – sealed containment facility where experiments are carried out on the virulent fungus known as Draconian Red Weed.
18. Geo-thermal power station provides the base with an independent energy source.
19. Blocks R1 to R3 are maximum security and are believed to be hospital wings for the various human/alien hybrids found after the battle of Dulce Airbase in 1980.
20. British Science Block – houses an on-site team of British scientists working on the crashed black triangle ship transferred from the UK in the early 1980s.
21. Auntie May's Alien Café – this military-owned diner is virtually unchanged from when it opened in the 1950s; it's the main social hub for the base and welcomes all species in an informal setting.

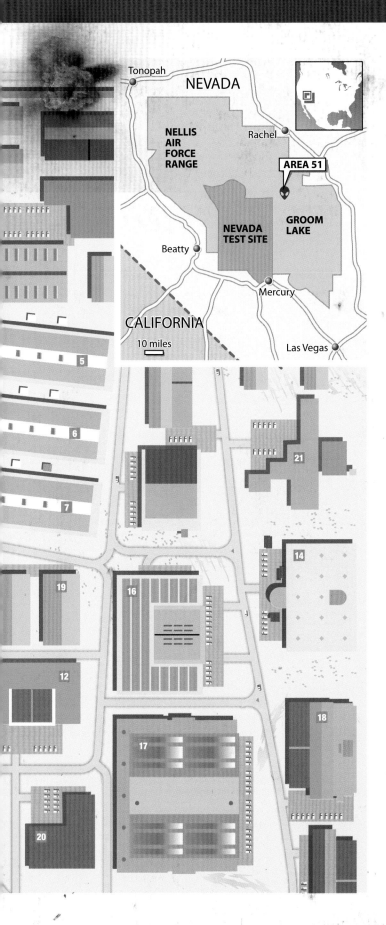

THE TREATY OF GREADA

This treaty signed by President Dwight Eisenhower in 1954 was the first formal agreement between humanity and an alien species. By the time the President met the Grey delegation for a face-to-face meeting, the Greys had been on Earth for a number of years and had already exchanged intelligence on other alien species as a demonstration of their goodwill towards humanity.

It's difficult now to ascertain whether the President felt coerced into an agreement with the Greys – clearly far more advanced than any life form on Earth – or decided that it was the best path to avoid inter-planetary conflict. The essence of the treaty was to offer the Greys permission to abduct several thousand humans per Earth year, provided that the individuals were returned and they were unharmed by the process.

In addition, the Greys were allowed to establish their own research facilities at Dulce Airbase in New Mexico. The Greys were most interested in collecting human DNA but at the time their agenda wasn't fully understood. In exchange, the Greys agreed to provide intelligence on the various alien species that could threaten Earth as well as some of their technologies, including developments in stealth technology, the microprocessor and the alloy titanium. Humans were also free to work on the crashed ship from Roswell and spent the next decades attempting to reverse-engineer it. Once the treaty was signed, most Greys moved to the underground bunker at Dulce Airbase although a couple remained at Area 51 as advisers.

> THE GREYS WERE POLITE ENOUGH. THEY'RE KINDA FRAGILE-LOOKING AND CAN MAKE FOLKS FEEL UNCOMFORTABLE AS THEY SEEM TO BE ABLE TO READ MINDS. THEY CAN COME ACROSS AS A BIT VACANT BECAUSE THEY DON'T SAY MUCH. I SUPPOSE WE WERE AS STRANGE TO THEM. THEY FOUND US LARGE, CLUMSY AND NOISY. I CAN'T SAY I EVER TRUSTED THEM, NONE OF SECURITY MEN DID, BUT I KNOW ONE THING – THEY COULDN'T TAKE THEIR DRINK. JUST A DROP OF THE HARD STUFF AND THEY START CHATTERING AWAY AND MAKING THE WORST SMELLS I'VE EVER COME ACROSS.

SERGEANT OTTO RAINER, 422ND DIVISION, SPECIAL SECURITY OPERATION, DULCE AIRBASE, 1959–64

THE BATTLE OF DULCE AIRBASE

By the 1970s abduction levels reached an all-time high despite the US Government's agreement with the Greys to contain the problem. It became quite obvious that the Greys weren't getting enough humans for their requirements through 'official' channels, which restricted the volumes they could take. An FBI investigation noted a growing trend for abductees to be taken multiple times and, more disturbingly, there was an increase in the number of complete disappearances.

For their part, the Greys calmly dismissed accusations against them, suggesting that other alien races such as Little Green Men and Draconians were to blame. However, the US Government became increasingly suspicious about both the abduction numbers and the rumours of horrific experiments being done in secret at the Greys' complex in Dulce Airbase.

Finally, it was Jimmy Carter who in 1979 ordered that the agreement with the Greys be terminated. The US Government could no longer accept the status quo with the Greys, especially as military sources by now considered that the technological advances being handed over by the powerful and technologically sophisticated Greys in exchange were merely 'trinkets' and of little benefit to humanity.

> THE ENEMY WE ENGAGED AT THE BASE MAY BE DESCRIBED AS 'ALIEN' IF THIS INVESTIGATION DECIDES TO USE SUCH A TERM. THE COMBATANTS WITNESSED WERE CERTAINLY HUMAN IN FORM, ALBEIT WITH RADICALLY ALTERED APPEARANCE, POSSIBLY ACHIEVED THROUGH PHYSICAL MANIPULATION.
>
> **UNNAMED SOURCE, CLOSED SENATE COMMITTEE HEARING, 1982**

DULCE AIRBASE

1. Known as 'The Tube', this giant concrete cylinder was built to specifications given by the Greys and was used to store and launch Type 1 Grey saucers.
2. The Greys were working on a transit system using advanced laser-technology before the base closed.
3. The top floor contained a mixture of human and Grey security guards.
4. The laboratory level was opened to human audit on several occasions but contained no hint as to the horrific genetic experiments that were being carried out on the lower levels.
5. The alien housing level was sealed and had a specially created artificial atmosphere and gravity.
6. The lower levels were destroyed during the fighting in 1980 and, according to witnesses, were scenes of both carnage and some freakish mutations. Once cleared, these levels were sealed by the US Government.

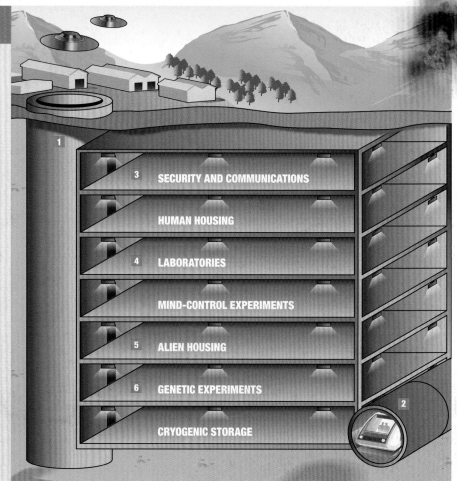

3 SECURITY AND COMMUNICATIONS

HUMAN HOUSING

4 LABORATORIES

MIND-CONTROL EXPERIMENTS

5 ALIEN HOUSING

6 GENETIC EXPERIMENTS

CRYOGENIC STORAGE

THE BATTLE

After it became clear that the Greys didn't intend to leave Dulce Airbase, President Jimmy Carter had little choice and removed them by force. What followed became known as the Battle of Dulce Airbase – a nightmarish fight for the Delta Force and the other special forces deployed. Witnesses to the battle spoke of flesh-burning laser guns, disappearing opponents and – most frightening of all – many whispered of the hideous alien/human hybrid creatures they found on the lower levels.

EYE-WITNESS ACCOUNT

One of the Army Rangers involved in the action in 1980 has agreed to provide a statement on the battle provided his identity is concealed, as much of the information around the incident is still classified.

'This was a fight like no other and believe me when I say this. I'd been in Vietnam years before and I'd seen plenty there but nothing like this. When my squad arrived, the entrance was abandoned. There were meant to be around 40 civilian scientists and security guards supporting the Greys in their work. We never found a trace of any of them – not even an item of clothing. There were typically 10–20 aliens on site at any one time but with the lack of initial contact we kinda thought they might have already bugged out. But then the shooting started. It was mostly our guys firing at every shadow and blur they saw. I didn't hear any return fire but the man to the right of me fell. As he lay on the concrete floor I could see there was a large part of his chest missing – no blood, it was clean as a whistle, like a chunk had just been vaporised. We fought our way down the levels, hardly seeing the enemy, just fleeting glimpses. They seemed to be using some sort of cloaking device but we soon realised we could spot them by making out their blurred outlines. My squad lost 14 men in that fight and it was hellish battling through those tiny corridors. We recovered four alien bodies in the end, don't know what happened to the others. But it was the creatures we found on the bottom level which I still have nightmares about.

CENSORED
WORDS DEEMED TOO SHOCKING FOR PUBLICATION

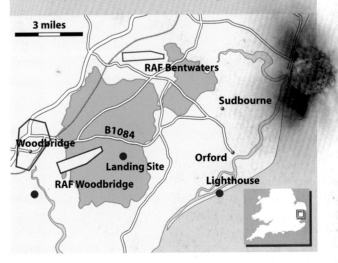

▶ A BRITISH ROSWELL?

The UFO crash just outside RAF Woodbridge in Suffolk, England, in late December 1980 is the most well-known alien incident in the UK, with dozens of eye-witness statements over a period of about a week. Until this incident, the Ministry of Defence and the RAF had been open about 'official' encounters with unidentified objects; for example, they released full transcripts of the so-called North Downs Landing near Wye in Kent in 1966. However, RAF Woodbridge was leased to the US Air Force at the time of the alien incident and there was never an official investigation into the alleged crash despite pressure from the British public. The only UK statement released was by the Chief of Defence Staff, Lord Peter Hill-Norton, who stated: 'Whatever happened at this USAF base was necessarily of national security interest.' This was a curious and cryptic phrase.

KEY EVENTS AT RENDLESHAM FOREST

▶ Throughout December 1980, there were reports from across the area of lights in the sky.

▶ The most controversial episode occurred on 27 December. A member of the US Air Force went public in 1997 about what he witnessed that day, claiming that American forces fired missiles at and brought down 'a dark, triangular-shaped vessel of unknown origin'. Official sources stated that they didn't open fire on any airborne object and denied the existence of any ground-to-air missiles at the base.

▶ For 28–30 December, the whole base was on lockdown, with local roads closed and flights diverted.

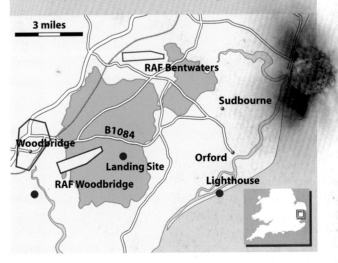

A HISTORY OF ALIEN CONTACT

THE POST-ROSWELL ERA (1980 ONWARDS)

Since the collapse of the Treaty of Greada in 1980, humanity has been in a *de facto* 'cold war' with the Greys. They and other species have continued to visit our planet and now, more than ever, we fear that it's only a matter of time before they come in force and to conquer. We have learned much from the Greys and a significant proportion of the information in this book has been sourced via Grey intelligence. But, as humans, we're more united than ever against the alien threat. Via the United Nations, countries exchange intelligence and cooperate far more.

We now know that aliens have been visiting Earth for tens of thousands of years; in fact, we have numerous documented accounts of their intervention in human affairs as far back at the Sumerian encounters around 3000 BC. However, the key events of the post-Roswell era, as summarised in the timeline below, indicate the heightened threat we now face. The timeline presents an overview – there have been hundreds more encounters or crashes – by focusing on the main incidents that have sculpted our relationship with aliens and our current exposure to hostile invasion.

'It is clear to the members of this committee that our nation now faces a dual threat. Firstly, the forces of red communism surround us on every side, working in cloaked secrecy to bring about the destruction of our democratic tradition and institutions. Secondly, there are those unknown forces from beyond our world which we have discussed during this investigation and which can field military technology eons ahead of our own. In conclusion, whilst the first may be the most immediate and obvious threat, it is the second which most concerns us. We would strongly recommend moving to gain a United Nations Resolution on this issue as soon as is practical.

▄▄▄▄▄▄▄▄▄▄▄▄▄▄▄▄▄▄▄
▄▄▄▄▄▄▄▄▄▄▄▄▄▄▄▄▄▄▄
▄▄▄▄▄▄▄▄▄▄▄▄▄▄▄▄▄▄▄
▄▄▄▄▄▄▄▄▄▄▄▄▄▄▄▄▄▄▄
▄▄▄▄▄▄▄▄▄▄▄▄▄▄▄▄▄▄▄   14/05
▄▄▄▄▄▄▄▄▄▄▄▄▄▄▄▄▄▄▄   CP

Summary Report, Closed Senate Committee Hearing, November 1982, Volume 2, Pages 12–13, Presidential Summary

1980	1982	1983	1984	1985
A black triangle ship crashes near RAF Woodbridge and is recovered by the British and nearby American air force personnel. The Ministry of Defence covers up all evidence but a ship is recovered along with the bodies of three Little Green Men. The RAF Woodbridge incident is known as the 'British Roswell'. This incident led to the creation of the Ministry of Alien Defence to protect the UK; its first office is above Tiny Tim's tea shop in Canterbury.	A UFO flew over Soviet airspace and the nuclear missiles of the Byelokoroviche airbase in the Ukraine. Twenty R-12 missiles were programmed and targeted by the unknown triangular-shaped vessel and only prevented from launching by a last-minute intervention from a senior KGB official on site.	▄▄▄▄▄▄▄ ▄▄▄▄▄▄▄ ▄▄▄▄▄▄▄ ▄▄▄▄▄ For legal reasons, Haynes Publishing would like to state that a cloaked Draconian vessel did not crash in Nigeria in 1983 and that three reptilian bodies were definitely not recovered and taken to Area 51. ▄▄▄▄▄▄▄ ▄▄▄▄▄▄▄ ▄▄▄▄▄▄▄ ▄▄▄▄▄▄▄ ▄▄▄▄▄▄▄ ▄▄▄▄▄▄▄	A Chinese frigate recovered a hexagonal UFO that was found floating on the surface near the disputed Sakhalin Islands. There were no aliens aboard but the Chinese government was convinced that there was a Draconian plot to take over the People's Republic of China and instigated nationwide checks, finding over 100 cloned officials during the first six months of investigation.	United Nations Security Council Resolution 1013 was a secret international policy agreed at the height of the Cold War that, should an extra-terrestrial biological entity survive a crash-landing, the country holding that being would assume responsibility for its interrogation and extermination. Nations begin sharing information on aliens.

MINISTRY OF ALIEN DEFENCE

A HISTORY OF ALIEN CONTACT
UFO CONTACTS SINCE 1982

The startling graph on the right clearly shows an alarming increase in the frequency of alien intrusion into our airspace. It should be noted that these figures exclude any contacts outside Earth's atmosphere. In addition, it is currently impossible for our authorities to detect cloaked vessels such as Draconian pod ships. This data covers Confirmed Contacts supplied by reliable military and government sources – these aren't reports of people 'seeing something in the sky'.

THERE WERE OVER 70,000 UFO SIGHTINGS IN NORTH AMERICA ALONE IN 2010, WITH SIMILAR NUMBERS ACROSS CHINA AND THE RUSSIAN FEDERATION. THE IMPLICATIONS ARE CLEAR. THE ALIENS ARE GROWING MORE CONFIDENT OF THEIR SUPREMACY OVER EARTH AND ARE POSSIBLY MOVING INTO THE FINAL PHASES BEFORE A MAJOR MILITARY INTERVENTION ON OUR PLANET.

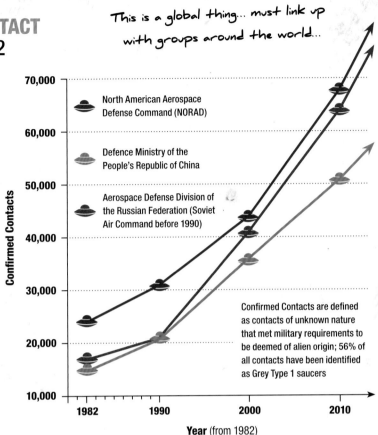

This is a global thing... must link up with groups around the world...

Legend:
- North American Aerospace Defense Command (NORAD)
- Defence Ministry of the People's Republic of China
- Aerospace Defense Division of the Russian Federation (Soviet Air Command before 1990)

Confirmed Contacts (y-axis): 10,000 – 70,000
Year (from 1982) (x-axis): 1982, 1990, 2000, 2010

Confirmed Contacts are defined as contacts of unknown nature that met military requirements to be deemed of alien origin; 56% of all contacts have been identified as Grey Type 1 saucers

1991

An Iranian diplomat in Iraq collapsed and started to 'melt like wax'. It was later discovered that he had no belly button and bore the telltale mark on the back of his neck indicating that he had been a clone. Unfortunately, his remains were destroyed during the first Gulf War.

1997

A student walked into the US embassy in Beijing claiming to have a message from the species we know as the Little Green Men. In poorly written English, the letter contained several very advanced mathematical concepts as evidence of authenticity. The note demanded the removal of all versions of the movie *Mars Attacks* and threatened the destruction of several cities if this instruction wasn't carried out.

2000

The United Nations Office for Earth Defence (UNED) was created as a separate entity from The United Nations Office for Outer Space Affairs. The new body was – and is – supported by the governments of all major nations and took over direct control of the worldwide network of 'Men in Black' units. Part of the organisation's brief is to gradually open the public's mind to the existence of extra-terrestrial life.

2002

The United Nations Office for Earth Defence published its core document, 'A Blueprint for the Defence of Earth', which includes the famous ET Invasion Matrix. It recommends that governments continue to deny the existence of extra-terrestrial life.

2014

NASA lost contact with the Spirit rover on Mars. One grainy half-picture appears to show a tiny green figure urinating on the rover. NASA denied these claims, citing 'excessive condensation in the circuits' as the reason for lost contact.

IT'S CLEAR THAT A FORCE FROM BEYOND OUR SOLAR SYSTEM IS CURRENTLY MONITORING OUR ACTIVITIES AND A SIMPLE EXTRAPOLATION OF THE STATISTICS INDICATES THAT THEIR PLANS ARE ESCALATING.

ALIEN CONTACT AND ABDUCTION

Although a surprise to a majority of the population, a full-scale alien invasion of this planet would in reality be the conclusion of hundreds if not thousands of encounters over the past few thousand years.

Perhaps alien races have always been watching Earth, keeping a cold, pupil-free eye on the development of the primitive species that live here. What we do know is that the 'pre-invasion' – a term used by ET preppers – has already begun.

This includes covert actions by the sneaky Draconians to take over the planet by stealth and the testing of our defences by the aggressive black triangle ships of the Little Green Men. The largest body of evidence, however, comes from the hundreds of thousands of UFO sightings and abduction cases that are being reported every year around the world.

ALIEN CONTACT

This is generally viewed as a positive experience in which a human is introduced for the first time to a life form from another world. The alien visitors will often go to great lengths to reduce fear or distress and the process is tightly managed from their perspective.

ALIEN ABDUCTION

This is the aggressive act of taking humanoids without their permission and against their will. It can involve painful experimentation, the implanting of alien tracking devices, or even cloning and DNA manipulation.

▷ ALIEN ENCOUNTER LEVEL

FACE TO FACE WITH ET

Based on the work of astronomer and UFO researcher J. Allen Hynek, the Encounter Level was first suggested in his 1972 book *The UFO Experience: A Scientific Inquiry*. It has been developed and adopted by the United Nations Office for Earth Defence to provide a scale of alien contact and was most famously used in the Steven Spielberg movie *Close Encounters of the Third Kind*.

> **IF WE ARE GOING TO RESIST AN INVASION OF OUR PLANET THEN OUR FIRST LINE OF DEFENCE MUST BE KNOWLEDGE. THE ENEMY WILL NOT WILLINGLY REVEAL THEIR PLANS SO WE MUST RECORD, CALCULATE AND ANALYSE, AS OUR VERY SURVIVAL MAY DEPEND UPON IT.**
>
> **ALBERT EINSTEIN, NEW YORK CITY**

ENCOUNTER LEVEL 1
FIRST KIND

- ▶ UFO sighted by a witness.
- ▶ Unexplained lights in the sky.
- ▶ Being buzzed by an unknown vessel.
- ▶ Witnesses hear strange noises or smells.
- ▶ It's estimated that around 62% of unconfirmed Level 1 sightings are either hoaxes or cases of mistaken identification.

ENCOUNTER LEVEL 2
SECOND KIND

- ▶ UFO makes a landing on Earth that may or may not be witnessed.
- ▶ Evidence of landing or burn marks.
- ▶ Possible effects on car engines.
- ▶ No alien beings are seen during a Level 2 encounter but they may be heard over radios.
- ▶ There were over 1,300 confirmed Level 2 encounters in the UK and Ireland between 2010 and 2013.

ALIEN CONTACT AND ABDUCTION
DEALING WITH HOSTILE ALIENS?

If they open fire, they ain't friendly – simple

In 2005 a level of hostility index was added to the scale to make clear the nature of the encounter – running from friendly contact established to a bad case of internal probing, extreme danger and high likelihood of invasion.

In the early 1900s, when alien science was in its infancy, it was safely assumed that any contact with beings from other worlds would be friendly (level 2) or at worst unclear (level 3). The fiction of H.G. Wells and others was just for entertainment. But the increasing hostility of contact from the 1940s and the jet age onwards has convinced over 95% of qualified alien experts that we can expect an invasion encounter (level 4) within the next few decades.

1 FRIENDLY CONTACT ESTABLISHED
Some level of communication or possibly agreed next meeting. No obvious danger to humanity, potential for longer-term contact.

2 FIRST CONTACT ESTABLISHED
Both parties acknowledge each other but only limited contact made. Neither species threatened and no violence used.

3 UNCLEAR ALIEN INTENTION
Both parties acknowledge each other but no dialogue maintained. Alien attitude to humanity unclear.

4 AGGRESSIVE ALIEN CONTACT
Threatened with weapons. Alien forces make it clear that they have no wish to communicate. Humans may be abducted; could involve fatalities.

ENCOUNTER LEVEL 3
THIRD KIND

▶ Visible aliens, typically landed or manifested.
▶ Aliens may be disturbed at a landing site.
▶ Some form of contact – planned or unplanned.
▶ Many reports coming into the Ministry mistake known species for new ones – with witnesses creating features they have seen in fiction.

ENCOUNTER LEVEL 4
FOURTH KIND

▶ Abduction either against will or by agreement.
▶ Boarding of alien craft.
▶ Examination and possible implant of alien technology into humans.
▶ The great majority of Level 4 encounters are hostile, with abductions making up the biggest tranche. Abductees may be held in a craft and taken into orbit.

ENCOUNTER LEVEL 5
FIFTH KIND

▶ Aliens arrive in significant numbers on Earth.
▶ Loss of life due to hostile action, which may be accidental.
▶ Evidence of invasion intent or open contact with humanity.
▶ Dubbed by ET preppers as 'Alien Invasion Day' – it's possible that a Level 5 encounter could be peaceful.

ALIEN CONTACT AND ABDUCTION

FIRST-CONTACT PROTOCOLS

Since the breakdown of the American treaty with the Greys in 1979, it's safe to say that humanity has no official relationship with any alien species. Since its creation in 2000, the United Nations Office for Earth Defence and our various international Men in Black units have tried making contact with various species such as the Nordics, but to date none has shown any willingness to establish ongoing contact. Recently a paper from the United Nations Office for Earth Defence conjectured that Earth may have been included in some kind of 'sphere of influence' whereby species such as the Greys or Draconians declare our solar system a no-go area for other aliens but as yet there isn't any real evidence to support this.

ARE ANY ALIENS FRIENDLY?

Throughout this volume, we have assumed that any alien visitors will be hostile. That's what all the evidence points to and that's what the experts currently think. However, we shouldn't close our minds to the possibility that we will encounter friendly aliens, those willing to help us and possibly even ally with us to defend the planet.

> IF ALIENS VISIT US, THE OUTCOME WOULD BE MUCH AS WHEN COLUMBUS LANDED IN AMERICA, WHICH DIDN'T TURN OUT WELL FOR THE NATIVE AMERICANS.
> **PROFESSOR STEPHEN HAWKING**

▶ OFFICIAL FIRST-CONTACT PROTOCOLS

SAYING 'HELLO' TO ET

The alien first-contact protocol is taken from the Ministry of Alien Defence operations manual and may be used where you encounter a species that appears to be friendly.

Preferably all first contact should go through the Ministry of Alien Defence or the United Nations Office for Earth Defence, but sometimes this isn't possible. These authorities have teams of highly trained first-contact specialists, but if you're up for trying first contact yourself then establishing a medium of communication is the first important step.

As a final word on the actual contact, be wary of misunderstandings. Aliens may not comprehend our emotions and if you're taken aboard a ship or touched in an inappropriate place, it may be better to just bear with it. There's such a thing as 'voluntary abduction', where a human willingly goes with an alien species.

THE UNITED NATIONS HAS RECOGNISED THAT PEACEFUL CONTACT WITH AN ALIEN INTELLIGENCE IS THE WORLD'S TOP PRIORITY AFTER SOLVING GLOBAL HUNGER AND THE ENVIRONMENTAL CRISIS. HUMANITY IS IN DESPERATE NEED OF AN ALIEN ALLY. ALTHOUGH MUCH OF THIS MANUAL IS ABOUT RESISTANCE, IF YOU GET THE CHANCE TO BUILD AN ALLIANCE WITH POWERFUL NEW FRIENDS, TAKE IT.

Type 1 Grey saucer – I think!

STEP 1
ASSESSMENT

Ascertain species and intent. Use the knowledge from this guide. Is the species one of those outlined in this book? Do you recognise the ship? If you can, take a position of cover and observe. Make no sudden movements and remain calm. If possible, avoid using a mobile phone as any signals may be misinterpreted.

ALIEN CONTACT AND ABDUCTION
ALIEN COMMUNICATION

Give up Italian evening class and find out where I can learn binary code

In communication, try Earth languages first – the aliens may have studied our planet and learned the language. The official phrase should be, 'Welcome to Earth. This is the home of the humans. We talk in peace.' We know it sounds strange but of the thousands of first-contact phrases this has been deemed the easiest to understand and translate. Don't be tempted to 'mix it up' a bit or introduce any slang – you must work to reduce the scope for misunderstanding.

▶ Many aliens have telepathic abilities, so remember to open your mind and 'listen' carefully for any messages. At first these messages in your head may be garbled and confused. Have patience and work slowly.

▶ If you find that you're unable to communicate with the visitors through language or telepathy, mathematics is your next option. Try drawing a simple shape on the ground – mark out, for example, an equilateral triangle – showing that all sides are equal. Or list a few prime numbers using dots. An advanced species will soon realise that you have some level of intelligence.

Remember that it's not just about the language – an alien may have mastered an Earth tongue but human concepts may still be a complete mystery to him. For example, Greys have no understanding of emotion as we feel it, while Nordics struggle to grasp our aptitude for creating war.

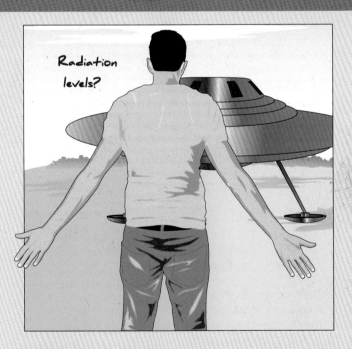

STEP 2
COMMUNICATION
Slowly approach the craft or the alien being, with your two hands out by your side and open, showing that you mean them no harm. This movement is designed to establish your 'peaceful' intent. If they vaporise you with phasers, you know they're hostile. If you're concerned about residual radiation, ensure that you're wearing tin-foil underpants.

STEP 3
OUTCOME
Don't become frustrated if you're unable to establish communication – essentially first contact is all about both species making it clear that they aren't going to exterminate each other on sight. If you have a successful 'silent contact', this will be something for you – as the technologically inferior species – to build upon.

ALIEN CONTACT AND ABDUCTION

ALIENS AND THE LAW

Let's be clear about this: Earth isn't a signatory to any inter-galactic accords and has no agreements with alien species to help us govern the behaviour of individual aliens on this planet. However, the Greys and Nordics have a principle known as 'Universal Species Law' by which it's understood that no alien species has the right to be on our planet without authority unless they first makes themselves known to us. For the Draconians this is a moot point as they consider our planet to be their property anyway. But under our laws here on Earth, you're fully entitled to take on any alien being you discover acting against the good of humanity, subject to the normal constraints of the law. Here are a few legal pointers to get you started.

1 BE CERTAIN A CRIME IS HAPPENING

Don't try to make a citizen's alien arrest unless you see an actual crime taking place – just because aliens are here, it doesn't mean you should spring into action with a golf club or cricket bat. They may have come in peace but your actions could start a war that would finish off our planet

You must determine whether or not a crime is taking place. If, for example, you see a human being hauled away or witness a couple of Little Green Men mugging a small child to steal a lollipop, then by all means get ready to intervene with the full support of human and Universal Species Law.

2 THINK BEFORE YOU ACT

Think very hard before trying to make an arrest or restrain an alien being – a devious Draconian may change form and make it look like you've just attacked an old lady. Other aliens may be armed or be ready to resist. In some cases it may be best to wait for the Men in Black or other qualified humans. If you decide on action, be firm but try to avoid injury to the alien where possible.

3 DETAIN AND CALL FOR HELP

If you manage to restrain an alien being, even if the rest of its party fly off in their vessel, detain the creature and call for help. An alien prisoner is invaluable to the security forces here on Earth so don't be tempted to do any amateur probing yourself. Deadly force isn't permitted unless the alien is a physical threat to yourself or others. If the creature uses any 'mind control' techniques you may use reasonable force to incapacitate its brain, normally with a big stick.

Call for help as soon as possible and, when the Men in Black arrive, ensure that you explain every detail you can. Use any witnesses you have to explain what happened. In the United States during the 1970s there were at least two military court hearings held in secret in which humans were accused by Greys of violent and unprovoked attacks, so don't be tempted to start applying any 'human justice' to your prisoner.

 THE FOLLOWING LEGAL EXPRESSION APPLIES TO ALL SUBJECTS OF THE UNITED KINGDOM:

Her Britannic Majesty's Minister for Alien Defence requests and requires in the Name of Her Majesty all those whom it may concern to allow the bearer to move freely without let or hindrance, and to afford the bearer such assistance and protection as may be necessary from other hostile alien life forms.

Any non-human life form should be aware that any harm to the aforementioned humanoid of Earth will result in the strictest sanction from humanity and the planet Earth, in accordance with Universal Species Law.

REPORTING AN ALIEN CONTACT

Any UFO sighting, first contact or even abduction should be reported as soon as possible. Don't be alarmed if a unit of the Men in Black turns up and conducts a face-to face interview with you. In a first-contact scenario you'll almost certainly be invited for debriefing at one of the sites of the United Nations Office for Earth Defence; in the UK this will be a Ministry of Alien Defence site, where tea and biscuits are often provided.

 Ministry of Alien Defence (MAD),
Office 233/44 B – Sean T. Page,
Main Building,
Whitehall, London

 ▬▬▬▬▬▬▬▬

 etattack@mad.uk

ALIEN CONTACT FORM 333/22B

Name	Number of witnesses	Contact details
Kevin Dwebble	Just me	London, England

Location	Event duration	Time and date of event
My back garden	One uncomfortable night	1.57am, 17th July

Level of encounter	Nature of aliens	Friendly to hostile 1–10
Too close	Grey coloured	5 or 6

Alien species (if recognised)	Sketch of species/numbers	Sketch of craft
X-files aliens		

Number of aliens encountered
3 or 4 – it was dark!

Number of craft/ships encountered
One silver saucer

I call them 'sky people'

Is this your first encounter with an alien life form? If 'No', please give details.	No, I have seen this saucer before. I spotted it last year with my telescope and I've seen it hovering above my house before.

Have you or a member of your family been abducted before? If 'Yes', please give details.	I haven't been abducted but my Grandad said he was taken all the time by the 'sky people'. They put him in a loony bin but I knew he was telling the truth.

Describe in your own words what happened.
Your account should be as complete as possible.

I was returning from a Star Trek special event at The Scala Cinema (only £4 entry on Wednesday night) & I heard a deep hum. I went to my back garden and a saucer was hovering. I tried to make the Vulcan symbol for peace but must have got it wrong as next thing I knew I woke up in a cold, sterile silver room. I don't remember much else but I now have some discomfort when sitting down and there is a slight bump at the back of my neck. I rang Grandad and he told me this was the work of the 'sky people'.

ALIEN CONTACT AND ABDUCTION

ALIEN ABDUCTIONS

This undeniable phenomenon continues to blight the lives of hundreds of thousands of people around the world. For example, an American government investigation in 1970 estimated that up to 100,000 people every year were being abducted, while figures from the People's Republic of China two decades later reveal that an estimated 175,000 people are reported to have been abducted by alien forces in northern China alone. Since the closure of Dulce Airbase in the United States and the current 'cold war' with the Greys, things have only got worse.

Billions of dollars are being spent on covert operations to restrict these numbers but one alien research body has estimated that more than two million people are taken every year and the total could reach five million by 2030.

MORE AND MORE HUMANS ARE BEING TAKEN BY ALIEN FORCES AND, ACCORDING TO SOME SOURCES, A GROWING PERCENTAGE AREN'T BEING RETURNED. FOR COUNTLESS NATIONAL GOVERNMENTS AROUND THE WORLD, ALIEN ABDUCTIONS ARE FACT AND EVERY EFFORT IS NOW BEING MADE TO STEM THIS TIDE.

FACTS ABOUT ABDUCTIONS

▶ Around 80% of abductions are by Grey aliens and involve transportation to their saucers.

▶ Our best figures indicate that over 95% of abductees are returned and that over half of all abductions take place from the bedroom.

▶ Around 60% of those abducted are unaware that they've been taken, many only getting hints through flashbacks.

▶ If you've been abducted once, you're eight times more likely to be abducted again. Members of your family are similarly at increased risk of being taken.

▶ Abductions are rarely isolated events and spatial modelling has shown that they tend to cluster in specific geographic regions known to ET preppers as 'hubs'. Recently the Ministry of Alien Defence has noticed the emergence of 'super-hubs', where hubs have expanded and begin to join up. Many see this as an important precursor to invasion.

▶ Alien abduction is a crime against humanity. It isn't the abductees' fault: they aren't alone as there are millions across the globe who've experienced the same thing.

ALIEN CONTACT AND ABDUCTION
HOW WOULD YOU REACT?

In the US the popular magazine *Health* broke the taboo around alien abductions by carrying out a survey, asking how people would behave if abducted. It provides a useful, if worrying, guide to the kind of resistance alien forces can expect from humanity.

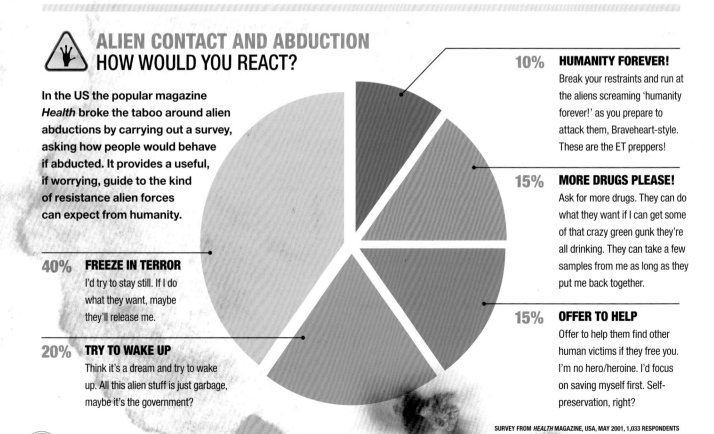

40% FREEZE IN TERROR
I'd try to stay still. If I do what they want, maybe they'll release me.

20% TRY TO WAKE UP
Think it's a dream and try to wake up. All this alien stuff is just garbage, maybe it's the government?

10% HUMANITY FOREVER!
Break your restraints and run at the aliens screaming 'humanity forever!' as you prepare to attack them, Braveheart-style. These are the ET preppers!

15% MORE DRUGS PLEASE!
Ask for more drugs. They can do what they want if I can get some of that crazy green gunk they're all drinking. They can take a few samples from me as long as they put me back together.

15% OFFER TO HELP
Offer to help them find other human victims if they free you. I'm no hero/heroine. I'd focus on saving myself first. Self-preservation, right?

SURVEY FROM *HEALTH* MAGAZINE, USA, MAY 2001, 1,033 RESPONDENTS

WHO'S ABDUCTING HUMANS?

Numerous eye-witness accounts have enabled us to build up a good picture of exactly who's taking humans. In abduction science, figures before 1970 are generally considered unreliable as various 'Men in Black' units during the 1950s and 1960s were routinely taking people they suspected of being abductees or alien clones, and in many cases these human abductions were mistaken for alien ones. Although such operations have now ceased, the image of these men dressed in black suits turning up to investigate strange phenomena has persisted in contemporary culture and fiction.

The Ministry of Alien Defence has conducted a major study into the identities of abductors and the results point the ET-like finger directly at the Greys. There's no doubt that other aliens are taking humans but in nothing like the same numbers.

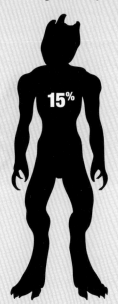
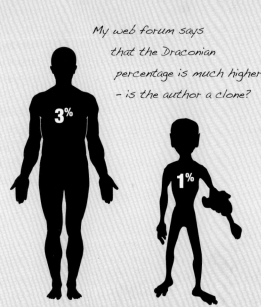

My web forum says that the Draconian percentage is much higher – is the author a clone?

80%

15%

3%

1%

1%

80%
GREYS

Their prime reason is the collection of DNA and the tracking of various genetic experiments over time. It's for this reason that people are frequently abducted multiple times over their lifetimes. As in any experiment, the aliens are highly persistent in keeping their data set complete.

15%
DRACONIAN

Theirs is a subtle agenda that involves kidnapping people they see as important in the development of society. Often the victims are brainwashed and have no recollection of the abduction. This makes tracking numbers particularly difficult. In some cases they deem the abductee sufficiently important to be cloned and replaced by an alien-controlled copy.

3%
(UNKNOWN)

We shouldn't discount the concept that other alien races are both visiting our planet and abducting humans.

1%
LITTLE GREEN MEN

There have been a few cases of Little Green Men kidnapping humans but these have normally been associated with accidental encounters rather than planned operations.

1%
NORDICS

Although not technically abduction, the shimmering dimensional beings known as Nordics have in some cases taken those they deem of exceptional spiritual ability to other planes of existence.

WITH WEALTH AND POWER CONCENTRATED IN SO FEW HANDS, IT HAS BEEN ESTIMATED THAT THE DRACONIANS WOULD ONLY NEED TO CLONE AROUND 5,000 PROMINENT FIGURES AROUND THE WORLD TO EFFECTIVELY CONTROL EARTH.

EYE-WITNESS ACCOUNTS

Still sceptical after all you've read? Well, close the windows and curtains, and prepare to read real-life accounts of some of the people who've been victims of the menace of alien abduction. These are all well-documented and proven case studies. If you're keen to read more, just search on any of the reliable alien abduction websites – you'll find thousands of similar accounts.

 ### SIGNS YOU'VE BEEN ABDUCTED

▶ You wake up in a completely different location, miles from your home with no recollection of how you got there.

▶ You experience unexplained periods of 'lost time' that can sometimes amount to days. Normally you don't find yourself with an unexpected tan or a new tattoo after a real abduction.

▶ You feel panicky and extremely emotional before going to bed. You feel afraid but you don't know why.

▶ You display symptoms of Space Adaptation Syndrome (SAS) or space sickness, which affects over 50% of humans who travel in space – these include dizziness and poor balance.

▶ You have flashbacks during the day or nightmares in which you're being experimented upon by black-eyed aliens.

▶ You discover an unusual implant in your body that professional medics cannot explain. Alien implants are typically associated with regular abductees. You may also discover new or unusual scars, or even notice the odd body part going missing.

▶ Under hypnosis, you reveal incredible levels of detail about the interior of a Grey saucer or the aliens themselves.

YOU DEVELOP AN UNEXPLAINED PHOBIA OR AVERSION FOR ANYTHING SURGICAL OR CLINICAL. IN SOME CASES, ABDUCTEES CANNOT VISIT THE DENTIST OR DOCTOR. THEY COMPLAIN OF THE CLINICAL SMELL AND OF FEELING UNCOMFORTABLE IN THE STERILE WHITE CONDITIONS.

REPORT 778/333/KHH
ABDUCTION LEVEL 3
SYDNEY, AUSTRALIA

'I woke up staring into these deep black eyes. I tried to scream but my mouth didn't move. I soon found my whole body was paralysed. There were more creatures around me and I could hear a dull mechanical drone in the background. I could hear them talking in my head. A dialogue was taking place. Images of beaches kept coming into my mind. They were just popping up there like a slideshow. Crude pictures of scenery in which something was always somehow wrong. One had a mountain with snow at the bottom but the peak covered with bright, blooming flowers.

I blacked out again. The next thing I remember was waking up by the roadside. I was still in my pyjamas. I later learned I was 50 miles from my home and I'd been missing for three days. I still get flashbacks to that night and I have woken up outside since then but have no idea how I got there. The worst thing is not being able to fight back – you feel like such a victim.'

REPORT 344/566/KPP
ABDUCTION LEVEL 5 (ABORTED)
HONG KONG, CHINA

17/02
Sr

The next thing I knew I woke up in a cold glutinous liquid. At first I panicked as I felt something down my throat. I pulled hard and yanked out a slimy cord. It was long and must have reached into my stomach or lungs. I gagged hard before pushing myself up and through a thin membrane-like cover. The gooey liquid surrounding me stung my eyes as I tried to wipe it away. As my vision cleared, I could see two pod-like beds on either side of the one I was on. In one was laid the blurry image of a massive dragon-like humanoid. The other had a reddish-pink human figure. I climbed out of the pod, pulling several cables from my body, and ran. I don't remember how I got out but I remember a ramp.'

LEVELS OF ABDUCTION

The experience of thousands of abductees has allowed the development of a list to help gauge the severity of an alien abduction. We believe that well over 97% of all abductions fit into one or more of these categories.

1 AN ENCOUNTER

An unprepared human may be 'buzzed' by a flying saucer, their car may be immobilised, their home probed and scanned. An encounter may be random or planned by the aliens. For the human, it's a frightening and mysterious event, perhaps with a dark portend for the future.

2 TAKEN ABOARD

Aliens will either enter the home or take a human from their location by force. Greys will often use mind control on the abductee and a tractor beam to lift the 'body' into their saucer. Draconians will often kidnap their victims while they are shape-shifting and appear humanoid.

3 SURGICAL PROCEDURE

The key difference between a Level 2 and Level 3 abduction is that whereas an examination may be completed during Level 2, including some uncomfortable probing, Level 3 always involves a surgical procedure. This could range from the insertion of a cloning tube to the removal of skin or organ samples.

4 PROCEDURE INVOLVING AN IMPLANT

Importantly, an abduction is rated at Level 4 when the aliens discover something of interest in their subject. Before a human is returned, he or she is implanted with a device to facilitate recapture and further data collection.

5 DISAPPEARANCE OR CLONING

Statistically, very few abductees completely disappear. Those picked up by Greys are normally part of a larger data set that the aliens are keen to maintain. Draconian abductees have a higher chance of disappearing, particularly if they've been selected for cloning.

WE WILL LATER LEARN HOW TO TURN A ROOM INTO A SAFE ROOM, WHICH WILL SIGNIFICANTLY REDUCE THE CHANCES OF A SUCCESSFUL ABDUCTION. AS TERRIFYING AS IT ALL SOUNDS, BE AWARE THAT THERE ARE MEASURES YOU CAN TAKE TO DEFEND YOURSELF AGAINST AN ALIEN ABDUCTION.

REPORT 211/994/KLO
ABDUCTION LEVEL 4
LONDON, UK

The following statement was made to the Ministry of Alien Defence with the agreement that the name of the abductee would never be revealed. The target was a British-Pakistani with a rare genetic and blood disorder that the Greys will do anything to examine.

'The first time they took me I was 15 years old. I was in Pakistan walking around our village and must have just blacked out. When I woke up I was inside a metal room surrounded by creatures. That's all I can remember. Since then, they've come every few months. Always the same thing. I just wake up on board their ship. They take blood then try to feed me some kind of green gunk. In 1991 I moved to England to pursue my legal studies and I was sure they'd never find me but they did. In a busy city of millions of people, they still found me and took me. I was beginning to think there was no hope. Then I noticed a small lump on the side of my neck. I was worried it was cancer but when I had it removed it proved to be a tiny metal tablet. A lady from the Ministry of Alien Defence took it and, touch wood, I've not had a problem since.'

It was obvious to the Ministry that the Greys took a zealous interest in this victim because of the rare genetic mutation he carries. The Greys are fascinated by our genetic diversity and the spontaneity of our genetic patterns. They were clearly tracking this man for decades until we removed the implant.

ALIEN IMPLANTS

When alien-defence experts talk about 'implants', they're referring to the devices extra-terrestrials have hidden inside humans for at least 100 years. The earliest reported implant was discovered in 1885 by Dr Thomas Clark at Colney Hatch Lunatic Asylum in North London. We still have some notes from the original medical report.

'Patient 4433 collapsed last night with more seizures. The orderlies reported that he was once more ranting about grey monsters and being taken to "the flying castle". I completed my autopsy this morning, finding much as one would expect of a drunken vagabond of the lower classes. As light streamed through the mortuary window I noticed a tiny reflection from the cadaver as it lay face-down on the slab and for just an instant I thought I caught sight of a flickering red flame, emitting from the back of the neck. Upon investigation, I extracted the minutest little mechanical item – pill-like in size and with a tiny red light. It measured less than half an inch but did indeed seem to have workings or markings on it. I placed it in a metal dish and asked one of the orderlies to call for Dr Smith. However, he was destined never to view the object. No sooner had it been left in the air than it fizzled and dissolved as if it had been placed in acid.'
Medical Notes of Dr Thomas Clark, Volume IV, May 1885

▶ TYPES OF ALIEN IMPLANT

GREY OR DRACONIAN?

There are three main types of implant and it's believed that only the Greys and the Draconians currently operate them. Little is known of the nano-mechanics behind implants as most seem to 'auto-destruct' when removed from their human host. Typically, they're found in people who've reported abductions, but not all abductees are implanted. To further complicate the picture, a number of people found to have implants had no recollection of abduction, their implants being found during routine medical examination or operations.

⚠ ADVICE ON REMOVAL

REMOVING AN IMPLANT IS NO GUARANTEE THAT THE ALIENS WILL NOT SIMPLY ABDUCT YOU AND RE-IMPLANT AN IMPROVED VERSION. IF YOU HAVE BEEN IMPLANTED WITH A DRACONIAN 'SMILEY', IT IS LIKELY THAT YOU ARE ALREADY TARGETED BY THE ALIENS. SIMPLY REMOVING IT WILL NOT STOP THEM COMING BACK TO FIND YOU. THE BEST POLICY IS TO REMOVE IT AND THEN CHANGE YOUR IDENTITY AS YOU WILL BE ON A LIST SOMEWHERE AS A POTENTIAL POD-CLONING VICTIM.

Make appointment to see Dr Patel

STARFISH
ORIGIN Grey
PURPOSE DNA tracking/unknown
DESCRIPTION Star-like implant; will be found throughout the body.

SILVER
ORIGIN Grey
PURPOSE DNA tracking
DESCRIPTION Pill-like implant; can be found at the base of the neck or behind the ear.

SMILEY
ORIGIN Draconian
PURPOSE Location tracking on Earth
DESCRIPTION A thin tab-like implant with 'smiley' face motif; found at the base of the neck or spine.

HOW DO I KNOW I HAVE ONE?

The simple answer is that we don't currently have the technology to screen everyone for alien implants. Alien technologies have doubtless become more sophisticated and it's no coincidence that there are now more reports of 'starfish' implants than the older pill-like 'red', which was more common in the 1960s and 1970s. Further research is still required into the area of implants.

Some implantees have reported improvements in health and stamina after receiving their implants, while others have complained of listlessness and headaches. It has also been noted that implants tend to follow family patterns: one recent Russian study, for example, proved that a family had been implanted through four generations.

HOW DO I GET RID OF AN IMPLANT?

Firstly, you should never attempt self-surgery to remove a suspected alien implant. If you find the faint outline of a possible implant, consult a medical professional as soon as possible. Once your doctor has cleared you of any 'natural' illnesses or claims 'never to have seen anything like it before', the chances are you have an implant, particularly if you've experienced abduction or someone in your family has.

In the past decade the internet has become awash with budget providers offering low-priced implant-removal services, but the recent scandals around sites such as www.removemyimplant.com and www.implants4u.com, both of which were shut down, confirm that proper medical attention cannot be achieved on a budget.

If you're looking for a premium-quality implant-removal clinic, go for one that's approved by the Ministry of Alien Defence. One such clinic is Budapest Implant Solutions (BIS), which has operated in Hungary since 2009 and has become a centre of excellence for implant removal. However, be warned that prices aren't cheap: an implant consultation costs around £500 and basic implant-removal fees start at £3,000; removal of a Draconian 'Smiley' is listed at £5,000 plus. Discounts, however, are offered for families or repeat customers. Bizarrely, BIS sometimes offers Christmas or seasonal specials. Enquire in the first instance by email to: query@budapestimplantremoval.com. A referral from your medical practitioner will be required.

NEVER ATTEMPT TO REMOVE AN IMPLANT YOURSELF. IT'S A SURGICAL PROCEDURE TO BE CARRIED OUT BY PROFESSIONALS, NOT A PARANOID LUNATIC WITH A KNIFE.

WHY THE IMPLANTS?

GREY IMPLANTS

Grey intelligence tells us a little of their implant programme, although current estimates suggest that hundreds of thousands of us have been 'tagged' using implants. For the Greys, we're sure that implants are related to their DNA engineering work, allowing them to track human specimens either as control subjects or as part of some DNA manipulation programme. In tests, implantees have shown no particular genetic defect, variation or alteration, but of course this could simply be beyond our current level of science.

DRACONIAN IMPLANTS

The Draconian 'Smiley' implant is by far the rarest one. Perhaps the most famous person to be host to one is Russian revolutionary leader Vladimir Lenin. It's said that his autopsy was meticulously carried out in 1924 as the party initially feared that he'd been murdered. The Smiley implant received scant attention, with the medical experts reporting it as a faint tattoo. Only later was it identified from grainy photographs as a Draconian implant. The fact that such an implant was found in a major world leader provides a clue as to the purpose of these devices. The Draconian agenda is all about taking control of the planet and current intelligence suggests that these implants are used to track prominent people who are possible targets for cloning.

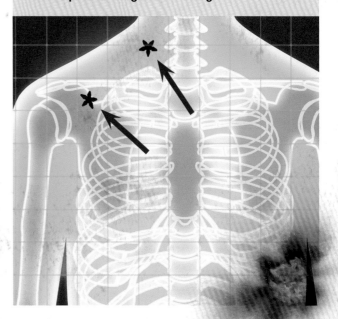

ALIEN CONTACT AND ABDUCTION

CATTLE MUTILATION

Humanity is not the only native species on Earth to receive the unwelcome attention of aliens. In the UK since 2004 an average of 5,000 animals per year have been reported as 'mutilated' by the National Farmers Union. This figure excludes animals that have completely vanished in mysterious circumstances. In alien research this phenomenon is called cattle mutilation as over 90% of the animals taken are cattle, although the figures also include horses, sheep and even dogs.

Cattle mutilation differs from any kind of predator kill in that the remains of the animal are typically found with surgical cuts, organs removed and with very little evidence of blood. Investigations show this is clearly the work of skilful surgeons using laser scalpels, but as yet we have no agreed theory to explain this situation. Initial evidence suggests that cattle mutilation is a worldwide problem, meaning that hundreds of thousands of animals annually are being killed by alien interference.

The current hypothesis is that this is Grey activity and their prime purpose is to collect diverse bio-matter from both the animals and the contents of their stomachs.

 PROTECTING YOUR HERD

Farmer Geoffrey Parsons of Somerset has spent many years working with the Ministry of Alien Defence after several of his own herd went missing in the long, hot summer of 2001. 'Our little part of the world has proved to be quite a hot spot for alien activity. There's something about the West Country that attracts them. So, wherever you are in the UK or Ireland – do what you can to protect your own animals.' If your herd is suffering from abduction, mutilation or any other ET shenanigans, Geoffrey's nine-point plan can help – it has been proved to cut losses by up to 100%.

▶ Have you noticed any UFO, particularly saucers, near your farm in recent months? If you farm close to an airbase you're more likely to see these ships. Stay vigilant, keep your eyes on the skies and learn to identify the different types of UFOs.

▶ Not every UFO is a threat to the herd. This rhyme is worth remembering: 'If black triangle ships pass, they're free to munch grass; silver saucer overhead, better run for the shed'. It's the silver saucers that go for the animals so keep a look-out for them.

▶ Ensure that all farm hands report any burn marks in fields. The aliens often check out farms before embarking on a programme of animal abductions. Have them report any unusual noises or markings they find.

▶ Keep a close eye on how your cattle behave. <u>Are they nervous or flighty for no reason?</u> Does your dairy herd have a 'vacant' or 'distracted' look? Have they lost their sparkle or is their milk sour? These are sure signs that they've been buzzed by saucers.

▶ Always have a firm count of the number in your herd. Don't leave the animals for extended periods of time without a head count. If there has been an abduction or mutilation, the quicker you respond, the higher the chance that you can protect your animals.

> ONE THING IS CERTAIN – IF YOU LOSE AN ANIMAL, YOU CAN BE SURE THAT MORE WILL FOLLOW. FIRSTLY, DON'T BLAME YOURSELF. IF NASA CAN'T FIGURE IT OUT, WE FARMERS CAN ONLY DO OUR BEST TO DEFEND OUR HERDS. SECONDLY, AFTER THE FIRST ABDUCTION ENSURE THAT YOU CLEAN UP THE 'CRIME SCENE' PROMPTLY TO AVOID THE OTHER COWS GETTING DISTRESSED.
>
> **GEOFFREY PARSONS, SOMERSET FARMER**

Make tiny foil hat for pet gerbil Kevin, he is vulnerable at the moment

IF BLACK TRIANGLE SHIPS PASS, THEY'RE FREE TO MUNCH GRASS; SILVER SAUCER OVERHEAD, BETTER RUN FOR THE SHED.

▶ Prevention is still the best policy. The saucers use a beam to lift animals into the ship. A simple tin-foil hat on each cow can play havoc with this process – for whatever reason it seems to interrupt the procedure.

▶ After your first abduction, ensure that all cattle are safely in barns or yards after dark. Don't leave free grazers out in the fields. Create a protected area if you have to, by working with other local farmers – usually they will have experienced abductions as well. Draw up a rota and work together to defend the farms.

▶ Try to obtain comprehensive agricultural insurance that covers 'stolen animals'. No insurance company will pay out on abducted cattle but if animals disappear or are eaten by a predator then a good policy will cover you.

▶ Be prepared for the stress and worry of working a farm through a period of alien attention. Typically, ET will move on after a period of a few weeks without a successful mutilation but this period can be hard work for any farming family. Stick together and work with neighbours to defend the herd – don't suffer alone or in silence.

▶ DOMESTIC PETS

MINISTRY OF ALIEN DEFENCE PET HOTLINE

According to the RSPCA, over 45,000 pets went missing from UK homes in 2013. Alien experts estimate that as many as 50% of them may have been kidnapped. Members of the public were so concerned about the threat of aliens to their beloved pets that a hotline was set up to support owners of domestic pets just as we at the Ministry of Alien Defence support organisations such as the National Farmers Union. However, we weren't prepared for the range of queries received, ranging from the worrying to the downright insane.

ANGRY HAMSTER OWNER OF DUNDEE

I'm worried that my hamster has been cloned. I saw it in a film and I know it's something the lizard things do. Could you come and arrest him? Blinky has been with me since I was a baby and according to my Mum is now the oldest hamster in the world at 11 years old. Well, I was reading my diary the other day and I thought OMG – he's changed. I looked at some old photos and, sure enough, he's changed size and even a bit in his colour. It's like every 2–3 years the lizards come and take him away and clone him. Why are they doing this to me?

While it's true that the Draconians (lizardy-type aliens) do favour cloning, we have no documented examples of them cloning animals, let alone your pet hamster. Our guess is that you should ask your mother about Blinky's miraculous transformations and his unusual longevity.

MEDICATED OF DUBLIN

Do the saucer people use animals to keep an eye on us? Last week I had the creepy feeling I was being followed but when I turned round it was just a pigeon. But, I don't know if it was me, but there was something 'suspicious' about the way he looked at me. Then only yesterday, I was walking back from the pharmacy after picking up my prescription when I was 'clocked' by two squirrels. I swear that they monitored me until I left the park. I think the aliens are using animals to observe us: is there anything you can do?

We have no evidence that aliens have used animals to monitor humanity. Their preferred method is via implants and cloning. In your letter, you infer that you're on some form of medication – if you ensure that you maintain the recommended dose you should find that the animals will return to normal.

BECOMING AN ET PREPPER

By this point, you may well be wondering 'what's the point?' Haven't the aliens, with all their power, already won? Surely we may as well just enjoy the time left until our new extra-terrestrial overlords arrive?

Only you can answer that question but read on if you're one of those who wants to open a can of whoop-ass on any would-be invader, or if you want to make them wish they'd stayed in their shiny saucer, or if you want to kick ET butt all the way back to the Dagobah system. If this is your attitude, then you've got the raw material to become an 'ET prepper'.

An 'ET prepper' – Extra-Terrestrial Intervention Survival Preparation Expert – is a person equipped with the knowledge, skills and tools to defend himself or herself against any aggressive intervention by forces from beyond this world.

At many of the conferences and meetings about the human response to an alien invasion, much of the discussion is around how our armed forces should respond and the strategies open to us as a technologically inferior species. As a consequence, much of the thinking and work on ET prepping has been left to a growing community of amateur survivalists who now see an invasion by aliens as a major threat.

> **THERE'S ONE GROUP THAT FORMS THE THIN BLUE LINE IN OUR DEFENCE AGAINST EXTRA-TERRESTRIAL INTERVENTION ON THIS PLANET. THEY ARE THE EYES AND EARS OF HUMANITY. YOU MIGHT CALL THEM 'WEIRDOS'. IN MILITARY PLANNING, WE CALL THEM HUMANITY'S FIFTH COLUMN. THEY'RE BETTER KNOWN AS THE ET PREPPERS.**
>
> **MAJOR GENERAL BRANT, BRITISH ARMY INTELLIGENCE ATTACHÉ, NATO HEADQUARTERS, SPEECH TO THE DEFENCE COMMITTEE**

PREPPING TODAY MAGAZINE SURVEY

A survey by *Prepping Today*, the best-selling survivalist magazine, indicated that the prepping community sees a hostile alien invasion as the second most likely cause of the apocalypse. This clearly means that those interested in surviving are beginning to take the alien invasion scenario very seriously indeed. In fact, according to online retailer survivalworlds.com, alien defence items are its fastest growing segment with a year-on-year increase in sales of over 27% in 2013.

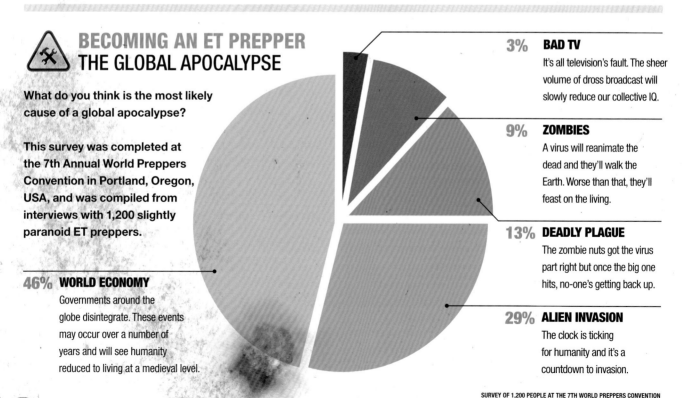

BECOMING AN ET PREPPER
THE GLOBAL APOCALYPSE

What do you think is the most likely cause of a global apocalypse?

This survey was completed at the 7th Annual World Preppers Convention in Portland, Oregon, USA, and was compiled from interviews with 1,200 slightly paranoid ET preppers.

3% BAD TV
It's all television's fault. The sheer volume of dross broadcast will slowly reduce our collective IQ.

9% ZOMBIES
A virus will reanimate the dead and they'll walk the Earth. Worse than that, they'll feast on the living.

13% DEADLY PLAGUE
The zombie nuts got the virus part right but once the big one hits, no-one's getting back up.

29% ALIEN INVASION
The clock is ticking for humanity and it's a countdown to invasion.

46% WORLD ECONOMY
Governments around the globe disintegrate. These events may occur over a number of years and will see humanity reduced to living at a medieval level.

SURVEY OF 1,200 PEOPLE AT THE 7TH WORLD PREPPERS CONVENTION

WHAT IS PREPPING?

ET prepping is not only about planning to survive an alien invasion but also a pledge to help your fellow humans in a fight-back against any would-be invaders. In 2007 an online group of ET preppers published what they refer to as their 'charter for the survival of humanity'.

▶ KNOWLEDGE IS POWER

Get yourself educated on the threat we face: make sure you know your Draconian Smiley implant from your Little Green Men ray gun.

▶ PERSONAL PREPARATION

Apply that knowledge to defending your person, family, home, community and planet against invaders from beyond our solar system.

▶ TRAINING AND VIGILANCE

Keep yourself fit, well-read and updated with the latest information, always ready at a moment's notice to defend our species.

ALIEN WATCH GROUPS

Once you start talking to neighbours about the threats from outer space, you'll be surprised how many will share your concerns. If you're at all concerned about being regarded as 'the crazy neighbour' then why not invite a small group round, watch a decent alien invasion movie, then casually turn the discussion to how you would defend your street if there were to be an alien invasion. Serve some good food and nibbles to create a relaxing ambience. Any group can start informally, meeting perhaps once a week to review any unusual activity or UFO sightings. You may use content from this book as discussion topics for each session. You'll be surprised how quickly you can turn a formerly 'normal' street into a curtain-twitching, foil-hat-wearing group of ET preppers.

ET PREPPERS: CALL ME PREPARED, CALL ME CRAZY, BUT DON'T CALL ME PARANOID!

▶ PREPPING LOGBOOK

YOUR DAILY ET PREPPING LOGBOOK

One of the most powerful tools in every ET prepper's kit bag is their daily prepping logbook. In this journal you should record every action or activity completed each day. You can schedule tasks such as patrols or make notes on curious observations that may be worth further investigation. If time is short, start small and keep it brief. Think of each entry as something you're doing for the whole of humanity and keep motivated. At any meeting of ET preppers, all should share with each other items from their daily logs – this can be a useful way to join up any sightings or unexplained activity.

TUESDAY	
Saw Mrs Wright buying a significant quantity of meat – possibly reptilian shape-shifter?	Situation normal – she just has a new dog.
WEDNESDAY	
Investigated UFO sighting in nearby woods/possible abduction attempt.	Complete form of the MAD in London. Leaflets to local homes.
THURSDAY	
ET preppers meeting – topic is black triangle ships.	Major headache following night out – possible alien mind probing?
FRIDAY	
Back bedroom is exposed to abductions.	Took the day off work/school and re-foiled the whole house. Local supermarket has now run out of foil. They call me the 'foil man'.
SATURDAY	
Alien Invasion Tutorial re-runs of Independence Day and Starship Troopers.	Copious notes taken and will test knowledge by writing an essay on Sunday.

BECOMING AN ET PREPPER

GETTING THE LOOK

Believe it or not, there are some members of the human race who aren't going to buy into the threat of alien invasion. Many are just happy to continue living their lives as if nothing is ever going to happen to our planet. Maybe they think it only happens to other planets and not ours? Maybe they dismiss the scientific evidence completely and just believe we can carry on regardless – oblivious to the fact that even now there are powers from beyond our solar system putting plans in place either to take our planet, make humanity slaves or – even worse – wipe us out completely.

For the time being you're going to have to live in this world of 'unbelievers'. This can be a challenge for a hardcore ET prepper – after all, you don't want to end up sectioned in a lunatic asylum only to be left in a strait-jacket when the invaders arrive.

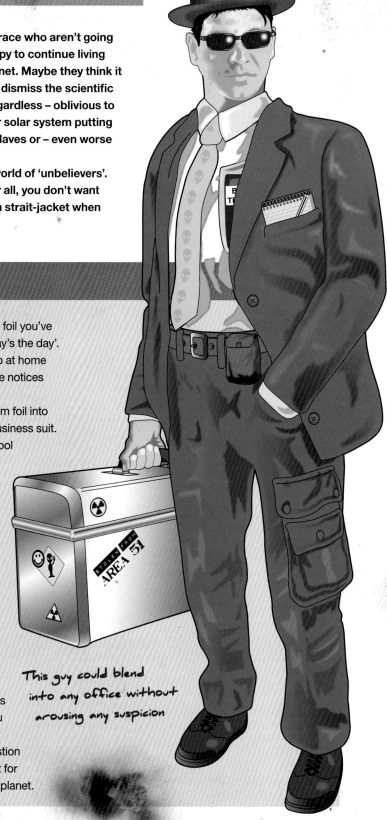

This guy could blend into any office without arousing any suspicion

▶ SIGNS THAT YOU'RE READY

1. You wake up every morning, look at the egg boxes and foil you've stuck all over your ceilings, and think to yourself – 'today's the day'.
2. You have boxes and boxes of aluminium foil stocked up at home and you add to them from various stores so that no-one notices you stockpiling them in such large quantities.
3. You're constantly looking for ways to integrate aluminium foil into your wardrobe, maybe inside your school uniform or business suit.
4. You've become known as the 'alien nut' at work or school but when taunted you just remain silent and cross the taunters off your 'must rescue from alien tripod' list.
5. When looking up at a beautiful night sky, full of stars, you don't see anything but danger – you know they're out there.
6. When you catch a humming noise in the background, your first thought is that you're about to be abducted and so you race to your safe room.
7. You treat new people cautiously and frequently upset newcomers by accusing them of being alien clones.
8. Films like *Independence Day* and *Mars Attacks* aren't enjoyable movies for you – they're training videos to be studied and you take extensive notes.
9. Halloween is a bad time for you, so you just stay indoors – there are simply too many people dressed up and you don't want to make any more unpleasant mistakes.
10. You know the aliens are coming – for you it's not a question of 'if' but 'when', and it frustrates you that people take it for granted that we can live in safety on this gleaming blue planet.

THE EVERYDAY ET PREPPER

Whether you're working in the office, going to school or just shopping at the local supermarket, the key to getting the everyday look is to combine safety and technology with an inconspicuous appearance and a nod to high fashion.

▶ A jaunty hat or beret will make you one of the 'cool kids' but no-one will ever suspect that it's lined with foil, thereby offering some protection against any alien mind probe.

▶ Dark sunglasses: no-one said being an ET prepper couldn't be cool – they might have thought it but they wouldn't say it.

▶ They look like normal trousers from the outside but on the inside they have a stitched lining of metallic foil fabric to resist any alien scanners. Man-made fibres are best, so you may want to consider purchasing a stylish polyester shellsuit to get a coordinated look.

▶ The pockets on these special trousers, male and female, are extra deep, with space for both caffeine and travel-sickness pills in case you get abducted.

▶ An anorak is best in black as some aliens find it more difficult to see darker shades of colour. There should be a pouch for travel pills in case you become ill during abduction.

▶ A built-in notepad is useful to record any suspicious events, ship sightings or alien encounters. You may wish to design a discrete 'utility belt' in which to store the various anti-alien items you want to carry. Find space for rubber gloves as you never know when you may need to take an alien sample.

▶ The male's standard office or school blazer certainly looks the business but inside there are several hidden pockets for a built-in Geiger counter, special sunglasses and a blood-testing kit – in case you need to screen for clones.

▶ The whole ensemble is made using the latest synthetic fabrics and polyester with proven protective properties against alien scans and their heat vision.

▶ The best footwear is a pair of blackened plastic running trainers, which look like smart work shoes. You need to be able to move quickly should an incident develop.

▶ The male's business case or school 'bug-out bag' looks normal enough but contains 24 hours' worth of supplies in the event of an alien invasion while you're away from home.

REGARDLESS OF WHAT YOU'RE DOING, FEW OTHERS SHOULD SUSPECT THAT YOU'RE PRIMED AND READY TO SPRING INTO ACTION AT A MOMENT'S NOTICE.

BECOMING AN ET PREPPER

ㄱㅍㅠㄸㄸ

HOME-MADE PROTECTION

Several alien species make use of mind-probe techniques to give them an edge against a human opponent. Apparently our brains are so complex and confused – by inter-galactic standards – that as a species we're particularly susceptible to mind invasions. Some aliens, such as the Greys, have a natural ability to 'read thoughts' while others, such as the Draconians, rely on sophisticated equipment.

It has been shown that both species can read minds within a distance of 100 metres, which means that you could be wandering down the street totally unaware that an alien is quietly picking your anti-abduction defence plans. Worse still, we can confirm that aliens can also implant 'ideas' into your brain. So, if you ever find yourself clearing a saucer landing zone in your garden and wonder what you're doing – the chances are that you've had an idea implanted.

THERE ARE MANY TOOLS AND TECHNIQUES YOU CAN USE TO PROTECT YOUR GREY MATTER – FOIL, MUSIC, SUNGLASSES. LEARN THEM AND NEVER LET YOUR GUARD DOWN. IF YOU SEE SOMEONE LOOKING AT YOU STRANGELY, JUST SMILE AND PULL THAT FOIL HAT DOWN A LITTLE LOWER.

▶ HOW TO MAKE AN ANTI-MIND-PROBE HAT

Humanity's defence against mind-probe techniques is typically low-tech and comes in the form of our remarkable ally – aluminium foil. A simple foil covering cannot guarantee that you won't be probed but it does ensure that you're as resistant as you can be. In Ministry of Alien Defence assessments, a foil covering of at least 0.6mm thickness was found to reduce susceptibility by over 84%, while use of heavy-duty foil of at least 0.9mm will offer even greater protection.

The advantages of wearing a foil covering over the head, particularly when you're out and about, are obvious in terms of protecting your plans and schemes to resist an alien invasion. Even when an invasion has begun, it's worthwhile keeping your thoughts secret from those trying to take our planet from us. Luckily, with the re-emergence of hats as a fashion item, you need no longer be considered 'weird' as you can easily disguise your foil covering.

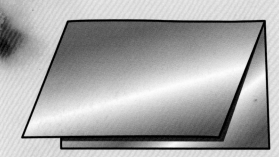

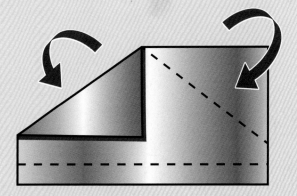

STEP 1

Fold the piece of foil in half, so you have a rectangular section with the long folded edge at the top. Use a smaller sheet to create a child's version. If you have a very large head, you may need to use two sheets taped together.

STEP 2

Fold the two corners as in the diagram so that the edges meet to form two triangles. Ensure that the shiny side is facing outwards as this has been shown to give a slightly improved level of protection.

MINISTRY OF ALIEN DEFENCE

BECOMING AN ET PREPPER
ONCE THE INVASION BEGINS!

Once the invasion has begun, you can put away any pretences of normality – when cities are burning and tripods are marching through our streets you won't need to convince any unbeliever. Some of the more subtle tools of the hidden alien war can be discarded once a military invasion of Earth actually begins – for example, you'll be able to ditch the smart trousers or foil-lined skirt in favour of something more practical.

Remember, you may be travelling long distances on foot and sleeping rough as well as battling an unearthly opponent. Items such as foil-lined berets will become standard issue although they'll only provide limited protection against a sustained alien mind probe. The best advice is to go to an army surplus store and stock up to build a real 'post-apoc' wardrobe.

STEP 3

Fold up the bottom edge of the foil so that it meets the bottom edge of the two triangles. You may wish to tape down the sides.

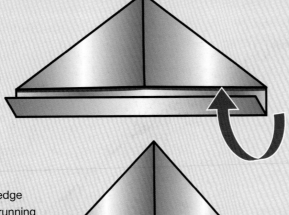

STEP 4

Fold up the bottom foil edge again, with the fold line running along the bottom edge of the triangle, and cut off any parts that stick out.

STEP 5

To convert this basic model into a foil 'innard', simply fold down the pinnacle of the triangle (never cut it). Tape it down along with the folded sections. You can then mould the foil into any hat style, such as a Bohemian beret, a businesslike bowler or a gangsta-style baseball cap.

⚠ **WARNING**

ALWAYS ENSURE THAT YOUR MIND-PROBE DEFENCE IS WORN CORRECTLY. AVOID THE TENDENCY OF SOME TO WEAR THE HAT AT A JAUNTY ANGLE – YOU MUST PROTECT THE WHOLE TOP HALF OF YOUR HEAD. IT CAN TAKE TIME TO GET USED TO WEARING A HAT ON ALL OCCASIONS SO IT'S WORTH HAVING A RANGE OF OPTIONS SO YOU CAN ADAPT TO FASHION AND AS THE SITUATION DEMANDS.

Ask at Playgroup about different hat construction techniques

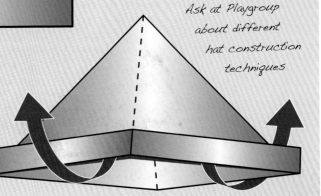

PREPPING FOR FAMILIES —

The best ET preppers are those who share their hobby and passion with their family. Obviously your starting point is to ensure that your partner and any children are aware of the risks out there in space. You may want to use some of the material in this manual to create fun games such as 'hunt the Grey' or 'let's see if we can find a Draconian clone at the shopping centre'. Be creative with children and sceptical partners. At first they may not understand your fixation with watching the skies, but before too long you'll have them all sleeping in foil hats and doing the kinds of things that are going to ensure that our planet can survive an alien invasion.

RAF PREPPING

Here in the UK, the RAF took overall responsibility for alien defence for many years, with much of the organisational material focusing on the threat from Mars. The RAF produced a series of leaflets throughout the 1940s and 1950s, including cartoon-type educational stories aimed at the young. This cartoon was published in October 1960 as part of the last such document, a 20-page leaflet curiously entitled *Communists Under The Bed, Martians Overhead*. At the time it fed into the hysteria over agents from the USSR and the paranoia about aliens from the 'Red Planet'.

Published by MOD Publications
RAF 1957/7/33A SE7

 ### BECOMING AN ET PREPPER
COPING WITH DISABILITIES

Do not rely on electric wheelchairs, the aliens can control them

A recent poll of readers of *Prepping Today* magazine showed that 35% of subscribers described themselves as having some form of physical disability. It's clear, therefore, that disabled preppers are going to play a significant role in any human fight-back in an alien invasion. A war against invaders from beyond our solar system will be a war against the whole of humanity – everyone will be a target for them.

> **THE ALIENS WON'T CARE IF YOU'RE DISABLED OR IN A WHEELCHAIR SO IT'S DOWN TO YOU TO PREPARE YOURSELF TO SURVIVE THEM AND MAKE SURE YOU CAN DO YOUR BIT, HOWEVER SMALL, TO SAVE THE PLANET AND HUMANITY.**
> **SHIRLEY 'JACK-KNIFE' COLLINS**
> **PRESIDENT OF THE COLORADO PARA-PREPPERS GROUP**

PLAN AHEAD

As a general rule, ensure that you have sufficient food supplies for at least 120 days. Stock up on any medical requirements and, if possible, develop a local network of supporting preppers. Looking ahead to a war against the aliens on Earth, think about the skills you can develop that would help humanity – perhaps you could adapt your house such that it could easily become a forward aid station, treating ray-gun burns, etc. Perhaps you could develop your skills in water filtration and supply our front-line units with clean water. Not everyone will be out there firing rocket-propelled grenades at flying saucers but that doesn't mean you can't play a vital role – particularly in ensuring that any human resistance is well-supported. If you really want to invest in safeguarding our planet, consider creating a fully equipped base under your home – complete with communications and maps of your area.

BILLY AND THE MARTIAN INVASION

Billy is at home ill. He can't believe he's missing cricket, all because of this stinking cold!

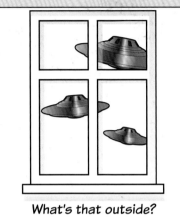

What's that outside?

Looks like flying saucers! From his window Billy sees that these Martians certainly DON'T come in peace.

The Martians defeat everything we can throw at them. Is this the end of England?

Then Billy remembers reading his science-fiction comics... he has an idea and it's a real peach!

What's this? Is Billy betraying the Queen?

Billy talks the Martians through his homework. They think they're top secrets!

But all the time he's breathing his germs!!!

Some of the Martians aren't feeling so clever!!!

Meanwhile Billy escapes using an alien jet pack.

The Martians are ill and soon start running!

The answer was in my sci-fi comics. I knew we could rely on our old friends – the germs!

BECOMING AN ET PREPPER

ET PREPPER PRODUCTS

The Ministry of Alien Defence regulates the many 'anti-alien' products that have surged on to the market since people stopped watching *The X-Files*. Some of these products are decidedly dodgy, but by working with various trading standards organisations around the UK since 2004, MAD has been able to remove from sale over 100 rogue products – everything from anti-clone chewing gum to an Insectoid binary-language phrase book. However, this work has proved to be a drop in the ocean as thousands of new items are flooding on to the internet market – a recent example is a farcical leaflet on inter-dimensional Nordic Wisdom and how to get ahead in the property market.

Be warned, there are some useful accessories out there to help you defend your home, family and planet against the aliens, but also watch out for useless products that could cost you dearly when you come to use them in action. Here are a few examples of some of the most popular rubbish out there on the internet.

RODDY GLASSES

What if you could help save mankind and look cool at the same time? Well, that's exactly what you can do with these new NASA-inspired shades. Using the latest hyper-glass technology, these cool sunglasses protect your eyes from the glare of the sun but at the same time allow you to see right through any Draconian shape-shifting. Regular Earth humans will appear normal but when you chance on a reptilian invader, trying to work its way into a position of power, you'll be able to see its lizard skin – and then you can warn your fellow humans. But with great power comes great responsibility, so use your knowledge carefully or you could end up on the Draconian menu!

'SEE THE REPTILIAN SHAPE-SHIFTERS BEFORE THEY SEE YOU!'

PRODUCT REVIEW 👍👍👎👎👎

OK, so these sunglasses do look pretty cool but they fail on every other count. They provide no UV protection for your eyes. We have no idea why they're NASA-inspired and, most importantly, they don't reveal shape-shifters. All round a fashionable but misleading product, although the snake-skin effect is pleasing.

ESCAPE-FROM-EARTH TICKETS

FLIGHT NUMBER	REPORTING TIME	BOARDING NUMBER

'PURCHASE A SECOND TICKET AND GET A FREE WINDOW-SEAT UPGRADE SO YOU SEE EVERY LAST RAY-GUN STRIKE!'

Are you constantly worrying about an alien invasion? Do you like the thrill of visiting new places? Well, escapefromearth.com may have the answer for you. Why not sit back and enjoy a guaranteed escape from Earth if we're invaded? Once safely aboard our third-generation super space shuttle *Aurora*, you can just sit back in your extra-wide leather seats and enjoy the fireworks. $200 per month per person doesn't just buy you peace of mind – it buys you and your family a fresh start on a new world.

PRODUCT REVIEW 👍👍👍👍👍

The subscription payments go through a Swiss bank account and all we can say for certain is that some rather unimpressive tickets do arrive if you start a subscription. This offer is an old-style scam. If you sign up to abandon your fellow humans in their time of need then you deserve to be fleeced every month!

ALIEN ABDUCTION INSURANCE

BMU* (Interstellar) Insurance

Cover: Full Time and Dimension

Name . . . .

Address . . . .

. . . .

. . . .

D.O.B . . . .

Insurance No. . . . .

BMU (Interstellar) Insurance is the trading name of Beam Me Up Insurance Services Groom Lake Road, Nevada, KXTA

The company will pay the claimant £1 per year until their death or for 1 million years, whichever comes first.

Check out our policies for alien pregnancy, alien examinations and death caused by aliens

If you're being taken regularly into outer space by aliens against your will, then you're sure to be feeling the pinch in your budget. Unexplained days off work, stolen pyjamas, missing chunks of time and the constant travel fares returning from wherever they leave you – it all adds up and could impose extra strain at an already stressful time. Help is at hand: the insurance industry has put together a 'total care' package. Just because you've been abducted, it doesn't mean your finances have to be!

BENEFITS INCLUDE:

▶ A guarantee payment for every 24-hour period spent in the alien ship.

▶ A daily travel allowance for when you turn up unexplained hundreds of miles from your home.

▶ A lump sum payment for any loss of limb or if you come back impregnated by an alien hybrid.

▶ Access to a 24-hour abduction support helpline for claims, manned by people who won't think you're crazy.

▶ A professional and discrete device-removal service, should a medical examination reveal that you have an alien implant.

'BUY ALIEN ABDUCTION INSURANCE NOW AND GET A FREE 'PAINFUL PROBING' PACKAGE, WHICH WILL COVER ANY THERAPY AS A RESULT OF AN UNCOMFORTABLE INVESTIGATION!'

PRODUCT REVIEW 👍👍👍👍👍

As ever, the devil is in the detail. The very tightly written terms and conditions of this insurance policy mean that short of an actual alien saucer landing and dropping you off in front of several witnesses, it's almost impossible to succeed with a claim. You're better off spending your money on hundreds of rolls of foil.

ANTI-ALIEN FOIL

Anti-alien foil is the only foil approved by both the United Nations Organisation for Earth Defence and the Ministry of Alien Defence. In fact, with over 200 square feet of aluminium and titanium foil in each pack, you'll be able to protect your entire house against any unwelcome alien intrusion.

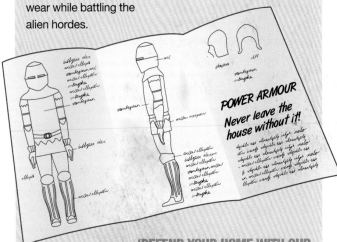

PROTECT'O'FOIL
Number 1 fashion accessory for conspiracy theorists around the world

ANTI-SCANNING FOIL

PROTECT'O'FOIL

The special properties of aluminum foil that shield the brain from being read. Also works nicely as a rain hat that gives the "tin roof" effect.

ANTI-SCANNING FOIL

But that's not all. With every box of ten anti-alien foils purchased, you'll receive our free guide to making foil clothes. Inside *Alien Invasion Fashion Police*, a 25-page booklet, you'll find everything you need to know about creating anti-alien foil 'power armour' that you can wear while battling the alien hordes.

POWER ARMOUR
Never leave the house without it!

'DEFEND YOUR HOME WITH OUR UNIQUE FOIL AND CREATE AN OUTFIT THAT WILL EVEN HAVE THE ALIENS DOING DOUBLE TAKES!'

PRODUCT REVIEW 👍👍👍👍👍

Expensive, useless and little better than what you buy in any supermarket, this product is nothing but a money-making hoax. Neither of the organisations mentioned has sanctioned this product, which seems to be little more than particularly thin foil in a fancy box.

BECOMING AN ET PREPPER

HOME DEFENCE

If you're serious about ET prepping, then you're going to have to make some major changes to your home as well as your lifestyle. The first few days of an alien invasion are likely to be confused times, with crowds panicking and various military units trying in vain to fight back.

You may decide to hook up immediately with a militia group or head off to help other survivors; whatever your decision, a strong, fortified home base is vital. For starters, with a few careful improvements you can drastically reduce the chances of any abduction or other pre-invasion alien intervention, and, when the fighting starts, you'll be well-equipped to support the war effort and help guide human forces to victory.

BUDGETARY CONSIDERATIONS

If you've already been abducted or have a healthy fear of the phenomena that affect millions around the world, then you may be tempted to start spending whatever is necessary to 'secure your home' from the alien menace. But be wary: there are unscrupulous providers out there ready to help you spend your money on highly visual but largely ineffective and expensive adaptions to your home.

Take control of your finances by carefully budgeting income and expenditure. Earmark an amount for alien defence activity then stick to it. ▓▓▓▓▓▓▓▓▓▓▓▓▓▓▓▓

31/12 CS

▶ AN INSIGHT INTO ALIEN TECHNOLOGIES

UNDERSTANDING THE TECH

When the average home owner thinks of home invasion, they consider high-security locks, double glazing and burglar alarms. While it's true that some of these can help prevent an alien from breaking into your home, it's essential that ET preppers have an understanding of the science we're up against.

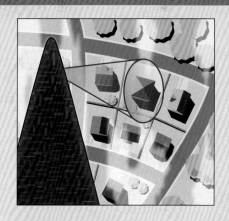

> EVERY ET PREPPER MUST GET TO GRIPS WITH WHAT WE KNOW ABOUT ALIEN TECHNOLOGY IF THEY'RE TO UNDERSTAND THE THREAT WE FACE AND DEFEND THEIR HOME AND THEIR PERSON. WE START OUR WEEKLY GROUP MEETINGS WITH A TECHNICAL BRIEFING: LAST WEEK IT WAS LASERS, THIS WEEK IT'S TRACTOR BEAM RESEARCH. ET IS HUNDREDS OF YEARS AHEAD OF US AND WE HAVE A LOT OF CATCHING UP TO DO!

SHIRLEY COLLINS, ET PREPPER

THREAT 1
SURVEILLANCE

Every alien species known to us makes use of surveillance devices far beyond our current level of scientific understanding. For example, we know that both Grey saucers and Little Green Men black triangle ships can hover high above locations and obtain a full read-out of who's within buildings, their location and more. We know that a layer of lead (at least 5mm thick) significantly reduces the surveillance ability of the aliens. Lead has proven to be a highly effective precaution.

THREAT 2
TRACTOR BEAMS

Many of the observations around the alien use of surveillance techniques are equally relevant to dematerialisation or tractor beams. To clarify, the process of dematerialisation involves the human victim completely disappearing and then reappearing outside his or her home. The way this happens is by means of tractor beams, which lock on to victims and bring them up into the alien ship. We have examples of beams lifting people out of rooms in buildings, usually through windows.

BECOMING AN ET PREPPER
SELECTING THE RIGHT HOME

Although no steps can guarantee safety from abductions or provide you with that perfect location from which to lead a fight-back against alien invaders, there are a few simple rules that can help.

1 LIVING NEAR PYLONS

It has been statistically proven that abduction levels are lower where a house is close to or surrounded by power or telephone cables. It's believed that any electrical interference can disrupt the alien teleportation system, meaning that the ship is forced to make a landing and complete a manual extraction – which is substantially more risky for the aliens.

2 PLAN AHEAD

You may not want to build an alien invasion bunker underneath your house but make sure you have that option – select a home on solid foundations with the right ground conditions for tunnelling. Avoid soft or damp areas and make use of any natural caves or man-made underground structures.

3 WHAT TO AVOID

Concentrated population centres are likely to become war zones in most alien invasion scenarios. Although you'll no doubt want to get into action in the service of humanity, select a home on the outskirts of town. Avoid proximity to any military bases, airports, power stations or major communication hubs.

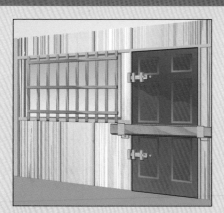

THREAT 3
PHYSICAL THREAT

All forms of electronic locks, alarms and other such defences have proved to be ineffective against aliens attempting to break into a home. To stop an alien gaining entry into your home, think low technology. Use the strongest possible metal locks and bolts, and back these up by barricading all doors and windows with wooden beams. Have your walls treated with aluminium 'wool' to prevent aliens from using their 'walking through walls' dematerialisation technologies.

THREAT 4
CLONE ATTACK

ET preppers often tick off many of the precautions already covered in this section, only to forget about the 'soft' form of alien home invasion: the use of clones to implant devices around the home. Clones often pose as repair men or similar, so be aware of the activities and purpose of any unfamiliar persons entering your home and monitor their work while they're present. It's worth insisting on a clone check before anyone enters your property.

KEEPING A PET

It has been shown that dogs and cats seem to 'notice' clones. It's by no means a 100% effective method but if your dog or cat goes crazy when someone enters, it's certainly worth trying to explore why.

The RSPCA has counselled against trying to put a small foil hat on a cat so this does leave felines more exposed to alien mind-control techniques.

Dogs are generally the best anti-alien pets and will happily wear a stylish doggie foil cap. Several ET preppers in the north of England have successfully trained ferrets, with promising results.

ABDUCTION PROOFING THE HOME

Preventing an alien abduction not only avoids the considerable physical and mental stress such hostile action places on the person in question, but it also strikes a blow against any extra-terrestrial plans for humanity. It's widely understood that the Greys are responsible for most abductions and their primary motivation is the monitoring and collection of DNA and biological matter. However, there are some who believe that they're also probing for weaknesses in species. They may be seeking to develop

a virus or bio-weapon to turn us into passive slaves – we just can't be sure. Making your home more resistant to abduction attempts is a good start.

Don't overlook the core structure of your home or apartment. A standard brick or wooden structure will be unable to take much punishment so, if you have the funds, invest in a reinforced concrete support framework to underpin the building. Sometimes older homes are more robust than newer ones.

STEP 1
DOORS AND WINDOWS

Aliens from a landed ship will make use of any easy access point, much as any intruder would. Despite all the high-tech tricks possessed by these unwelcome visitors, however, they have one significant weakness that we can exploit. Aliens struggle with wooden obstructions: this may sound low-tech to us but many of these civilisations stopped used organic woods thousands of years ago. Install wooden latches – not metal ones – on all doors and windows, and hold things together by means of wooden dowels rather than metal screws, bolts or nails. Wooden shutters across windows are effective at resisting alien technology and, of course, can look rather picturesque, giving your home that 'French rustic' look in summer.

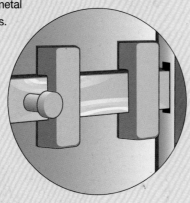

Try lining the walls with foil at night to avoid suspicion

STEP 2
EXTERNAL WALLS

Where you have cavity walls, these can be filled with standard insulating foam provided it has been mixed with aluminium or iron filings. It's also recommended that a thick sheet of foil be tacked to the walls – the foil can then be painted or wallpapered over. If you have solid walls, a thicker lining is preferable – at least three layers of metallic sheet.

STEP 3
ROOF AND CEILING

For about the same price as it costs to insulate your loft, you can alien-proof your roof and ceiling, giving you the peace of mind of knowing that alien mind probes and tractor beams won't easily shoot through. The standard solution involves layers of metallic foil underneath your roof tiles and inside the roof lining, stapled to the joists and rafters. Ensure that you use extra-thick industrial-strength aluminium foil. Aluminium foil loft insulation can be purchased at any DIY store and can also help reduce risk of condensation and penetrating damp – a win-win situation. Finally, put a layer of slate or lead across the loft floor for additional protection.

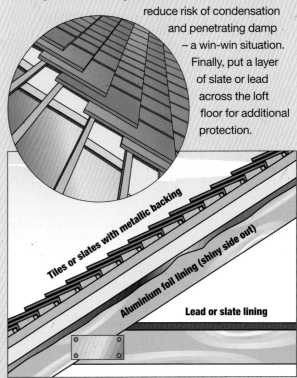

Tiles or slates with metallic backing

Aluminium foil lining (shiny side out)

Lead or slate lining

▷ BUILD YOUR OWN ALIEN SAFE ROOM

Where budgetary or time constraints restrict your alien defence preparations, you may wish to convert one room into an alien safe room. Even if you've alien-proofed other parts of the home, it's still useful to have a secure location where you and your family can dash if you hear the hum of a saucer. For those with a very limited budget, it's possible to convert a small wardrobe or cupboard into an alien survival pod – which is similar to a safe room but much smaller.

AT THE FIRST SIGN OF TROUBLE...

You should get to your safe room as soon as possible. Ensure that you have essentials – blankets, water and snacks – in your safe room as you should ideally stay there for at least four hours. Practise with your partner or family to ensure that everyone can get to your safe room in less than 30 seconds. Once inside, seal the doors and don't be tempted to leave until you're absolutely sure that any hovering ships have left.

INTERNAL DOOR

Door is fitted with wooden dead-bolts and wooden fastenings to fix it to the wall – don't let ET use his sonic screwdriver to undo the hinges only to see the door drop to the floor!

INTERNAL WALLS

Walls treated with aluminium-based foam and foil; this prevents alien 'wall-walking' and provides a practical base layer for painting or wallpapering.

SAFE ROOM

A well-stocked alien safe room, with thick lead and aluminium lining, and 24 hours' worth of food and water. Keep a few good books in there as well.

PREPPER DOG

A well-trained dog is the perfect early-warning system but once the bright lights arrive ensure that you take him in the safe room with you.

YOUR BED

Position your bed away from any doors or windows (with the walls protected) as these will be the next vulnerable points.

WINDOWS

Windows may be left clear during the day but a silver-foil blind is pulled down at night to prevent alien mind-control waves filtering in. The window is also fitted with wooden bolts.

CONSIDERING A NEW HOME?

If you're planning to move, ensure that you audit your next location against the information and advice provided in this manual. If in any doubt, ask your estate agent or the vendor about any anti-abduction features of the property.

NO HOME CAN BE TOTALLY ABDUCTION-RESISTANT BUT THE IMPROVEMENTS DESCRIBED HERE CAN REDUCE THE RISK OF ALIEN ABDUCTION BY OVER 70%.

⚠ WARNING

FOR STRUCTURAL WORK ON YOUR HOME, SUCH AS THE MOVING OF WALLS OR THE DIGGING OF AN ALIEN DEFENCE BUNKER, CONSULT THE LOCAL AUTHORITIES. IF YOU'RE RENTING, YOU NEED TO LET THE LANDLORD KNOW ABOUT YOUR CONCERNS. THE GOVERNMENT IS LOOKING TO INTRODUCE AN 'ET SCHEME' IN WHICH HOME OWNERS CAN APPLY FOR GRANTS OF UP TO £3,000 TO IMPROVE ALIEN-PROOFING AROUND THE HOUSE.

BECOMING AN ET PREPPER

THE PERFECT ALIEN INVASION BUNKER

So far we've looked at reasonably priced improvements you can make to your home to help you resist alien abduction or raids – lead lining will prevent the beaming out of your unconscious body, reflective foil will restrict an alien's ability to scan your home, and your alien survival pod may buy you some precious minutes if species such as the Greys or Little Green Men search your home. However, once an alien invasion starts, everything changes. Later in this manual we'll survey the most likely invasion scenarios in depth, but for now it's enough to know that invasion will involve a variety of assaults from orbital bombardments and attacks from alien ships to a full-scale ground invasion and even a war of extermination.

BASICALLY, WE'RE SAYING THAT FOR A MAJOR ALIEN INVASION OF EARTH, YOU'RE GOING TO HAVE TO START THINKING MUCH BIGGER THAN A FEW EXTRA ROLLS OF FOIL. THE ULTIMATE SET-UP WOULD INCLUDE THE CREATION OF A FULLY FUNCTIONING BUNKER COMPLEX.

▶ ALIEN INVASION BUNKER

1. Construction should be concealed. In a military invasion by aliens, the bunker will become a centre of resistance and intelligence.
2. It's recommended that a layer of lead and slate at least 10cm thick be laid over the top of the bunker. Alien scanners can detect underground structures but we know that this combination disrupts their readings.
3. The bunker should be equipped for your immediate needs but take into account that in the first week of an alien invasion you'll be joining up with other survivors to form an anti-invasion militia. Some of these survivors will come with their own weapons and bug-out bags.
4. A fully equipped medical bay to support a growing band of human resistance fighters.
5. Garrison bunk beds. There will be little privacy once your forces start to build up. Expect to have beds for at least 100 – by using 'hot bunking' this will mean that you can operate a force of 200 fighters as you take the war to the aliens.
6. You will need a well-equipped workshop for repairs to equipment and weapons. Make sure that you include a library of military and survival books.
7. It's good to have a secure examination room and a few cells. If you manage to capture one of the invaders you may be able to extract valuable information. Even alien bodies can be useful as human forces need to know how any invaders tick biologically – what are their vulnerable areas?

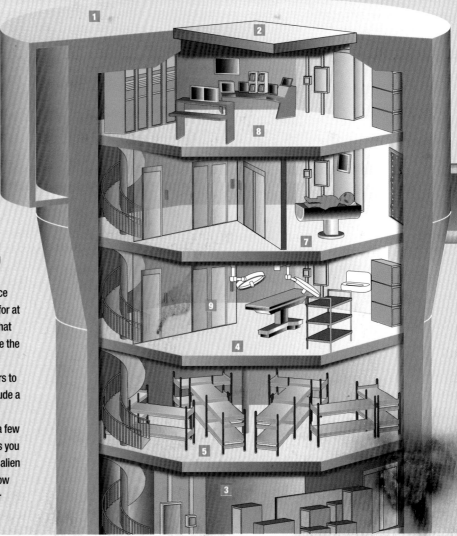

 MINISTRY OF ALIEN DEFENCE

It may be worth creating a dummy site – maybe with an exposed concrete bunker top and an aerial sticking up. Don't overdo it – the purpose is just to be a distraction. If it's spotted by an alien patrol, hopefully this will be the site they attack first, giving you a chance to go into lock-down.

Call the council on Monday – I need a home with a bunker

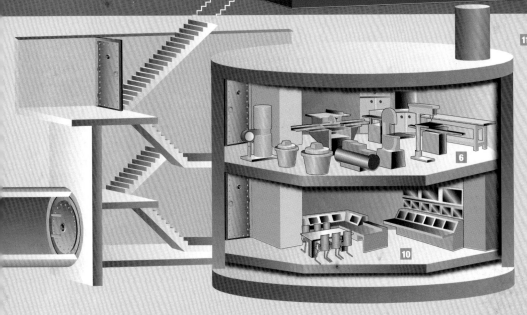

11 Radio Free Earth – while your communications centre will be abuzz with updates from missions in the field, contact with military units and any surviving government, the most important desk by far is the Radio Free Earth one – which broadcasts regularly to all survivors. You may need a more powerful system for this station to ensure that you can really reach out to people. As survivors cower in their homes while their towns and cities are destroyed by marauding tripods or unstoppable flying saucers, this voice will keep their hopes alive.

8 Command Room – this secure room should have a guard at all times and will quickly become the hub of any human resistance in the area. You'll need excellent maps of the local region; get large-scale maps and several of them. Ensure that you have maps of all underground infrastructure such as sewage tunnels or transport networks; any underground routes will be invaluable as the aliens can be expected to have air supremacy very early on. Humanity is going to need every advantage possible.

9 Conference Room – space to train your fighters, to update them on developments on the war, to debrief missions and to start organising the strike-back.

10 Communications Room – at the heart is a CB radio communications station, which can broadcast within a ten-mile radius to human resistance fighters, any remaining military forces and other survivors. It's believed that going 'low tech' will increase the chances of hiding the signals from any alien intervention.

12 CB antennae – a number of antennae should be hidden in various locations. It's vital that you keep broadcasting. As civilisation is shattered, humanity will become disparate, with military forces breaking down into smaller units and an outbreak of general lawlessness. Remember, any informative broadcast can really help to galvanise survivors and create a focal point for the resistance. Encourage the populace to call in with reports of any alien activity.

ALIEN COMBAT

In this section we're going to look at some of the fighting skills you'll need to counter alien aggression, be it an attempted abduction or a full-scale invasion. We'll look at techniques that can be used for physical combat with various alien species.

Hopefully you'll never need to use these techniques but practise them and be confident that you can battle the alien menace. Battling aliens isn't a new activity – humanity has resisted invaders for years. Back in 1946, shortly before his death, science fiction author and alien combat expert H.G. Wells offered the following insight for the future:

> IF MANKIND IS TO SURVIVE THE CHALLENGES FROM OUTER SPACE WHICH WE KNOW WILL COME, THEN EVERY ONE OF US MUST BE PREPARED TO DO HIS DUTY. IF RECENT DARK EVENTS ON EARTH HAVE TAUGHT US ANYTHING, IT IS THAT NOTHING LESS THAN TOTAL WAR IS REQUIRED FOR VICTORY. THEREFORE, I MOST HEARTILY ADVISE MY READERS TO EMBRACE ALL FORMS OF ALIEN COMBAT – FROM HAND-TO-HAND BOXING WITH A MARTIAN TO TURNING HIS MOST TERRIBLE TRIPOD WEAPON AGAINST HIM. I SAY TO THEM, SHARE YOUR EXPERIENCE, LEARN HOW TO FIGHT THESE INHUMAN OPPONENTS, LEARN HOW TO ESCAPE FROM ONE OF THEIR INVISIBLE SHIPS OR HOW TO ATTACK THEIR SECRET BASES. IF YOU ARE KIDNAPPED, FIGHT BACK. IF THE ALIENS INVADE, WE MUST ALL BE PREPARED TO FIGHT BACK FOR THE SAKE OF ALL MANKIND.

SOURCE: PERSONAL LETTER TO FRANKLIN D. MANNERS, GOTHAM PUBLISHING HOUSE, 3 AUGUST 1946

IMAGINE THIS SCENARIO

You remember dropping off to sleep in your cosy bed, or sitting in your car eating a sandwich, or even spending a penny in the bathroom – next thing you know, you wake up alone in a silver-walled cell or lying on a cold metal table surrounded by creatures from beyond our solar system. There's no way to break this news softly: getting abducted is a terrifying experience. Whether you're taken during 'peacetime' or during a full-scale alien invasion, the challenges are the same. You're held by a species that's far superior technologically and has dastardly plans. They're likely to poke you and prod you – or worse.

So when you wake up on board an alien vessel, what's your first move?

⚠ AN EXCEPTION

If you've been abducted many times, you may decide to do nothing, safe in the knowledge that your alien captors will simply return you once they're done. Maybe the odd bodily probing isn't an issue for you. But take into account that every successful abduction brings the aliens closer to invasion so you have a responsibility to fight for humanity!

STEPS TO ESCAPE

STEP 1
DON'T PANIC!
PULL YOURSELF TOGETHER

It's an old sci-fi cliché but in any emergency situation this is the first and most important step. This is a survival situation and this is where your ET prepper training will kick in. About 80% of the humans who escape from alien abductions do so within the first two hours of being taken or waking up, so you need to act quickly.

STEP 2
SURVEY
SURVEY THE SITUATION

Firstly, check yourself – are you injured? Have the aliens removed any major organs or attached any constraints or trackers? Scan your surroundings. If you find yourself on an examination table, try not to reveal that you're conscious. Don't suddenly start yanking any constraints – gently tug them.

MINISTRY OF ALIEN DEFENCE

HUMANS VERSUS ALIENS

From what we know of the various species throughout the universe, humanity appears to be a fairly large and robust one. Certainly in comparison to species such as the Greys and the Little Green Men we're both stronger and in most cases quicker. As has been noted before, both of these species see us as little more than speaking gorillas, but behind this insult there's an obvious fear that in physical combat we're actually quite effective. It would certainly take several of these diminutive aliens to take on an enraged human. However, the universe is a diverse place and species such as the Draconians are more than a match for us physically.

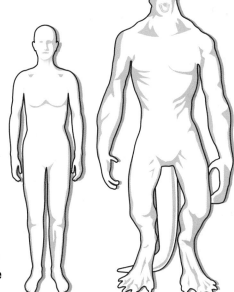

As a general rule, Greys and Little Green Men will avoid physical combat with a human. Draconians consider it beneath them but they'll fight if forced to – and will fight viciously. Insectoids? They just want us gone – full stop.

⚖ ALIEN-FU

Alien-Fu is more than just a martial art: it's a collection of techniques and knowledge that groups such as Men in Black agents have built up over the decades of battling the extra-terrestrial menace. Formerly known as 'ET-Kwon-Do', this is a unique fighting system that's now most commonly known across the internet as Alien-Fu.

All currently known martial arts are based on fighting humans but what if your opponent is a different species, with different strengths and weaknesses? Alien-Fu is our collective wisdom of armed and unarmed combat against ET. Only fight when conditions are favourable – remember, this is an enemy with overwhelming military and technological superiority.

Alien-Fu is based on three principles:

▶ KNOW YOURSELF

Your own abilities, fitness to fight, agility, etc. Most will never get the chance but build your confidence to know that you can tackle a pack of angry Greys or a gaggle of Little Green Men.

▶ KNOW YOUR ENEMY

Know the species you fight, their strengths and weaknesses. If all you have is a hammer, everything is a nail. Know where to hit different ETs where it hurts!

▶ BALANCE THE EQUATION

Your objective is survival first, victory second. This is about evening the score, which could mean grabbing a weapon, playing dirty and using tricks. This won't be a fair fight; you're not equal to your opponent.

STEP 3
ASSESS
WHAT ARE YOUR OPTIONS?

All the evidence we have gathered suggests that you only get one shot to escape, so take a few minutes to weigh up your choices and assess your surroundings. The most important factor is to try to establish whether or not you're still in Earth's atmosphere – if you are, consider making a break for it straight away rather than later.

STEP 4
TAKE ACTION
TIME IS NOT ON YOUR SIDE

You may not have all the facts but decide your course of action and work to make it happen. Adjust your plan as any new information comes to light and always be ready to spring on any unexpected opportunities. Remember, the longer the abduction continues, the higher the chances the aliens will get what they want.

ALIEN COMBAT

COMBAT AGAINST GREYS

Greys regard themselves as the great brains of the universe and are comfortable in their own superiority over humans. While it's true that they have developed over eons of history, their increased brain power has come at the expense of physical strength. Greys are small, wiry creatures, with over-sized heads and long limbs. It's worth noting that although their bones are small in comparison to those of a human adult, Greys are made up of a flexible cartilage/bone matter that's far stronger than one might expect. Don't just think you'll be able to judo-chop one of those matchstick arms and snap it.

Greys never willingly engage in hand-to-hand combat. They're comfortable using ray guns but aren't often seen carrying weapons. Their primary defence against those they consider 'lesser species' is to use their mind-control skills, so developing your resistance to their invasive telepathy is a key part of your preparation.

It's also worth consulting the several alien autopsy videos and pamphlets published by the Ministry of Alien Defence as these provide a thorough if gory overview of the biology of Grey aliens. Be wary of autopsy videos on unauthorised social media sites as they're often fictional and contain inaccuracies. As a general rule of thumb, if the pictures and video are grainy or black and white, then you are looking at a fake. █████████

8/02
hg

COMBAT AGAINST GREYS

THE GREYS AND FIREARMS

We know that most modern weapons such as air-to-air missiles are useless against Grey saucers, while the experience of fighting the Greys at the Battle of Dulce Airbase in 1980 also showed that firearms are of extremely limited use. Although Greys appear 'naked', we believe them to possess bio-metric implants that create a shielding force field around them to render firearms somehow 'inactive'. The current theory is that the aliens are using their telepathic powers to deactivate the weapons. During the battle of Dulce Airbase, some Greys did suffer bullet wounds but casualties were very few considering the amount of ammunition expended. Most injuries were inflicted during hand-to-hand combat.

> GREYS ARE PHYSICALLY WEAKER THAN US AND TEND TO PANIC IN PHYSICAL COMBAT, BUT IF YOU TRAP THEM THEY GET GRABBY AND SCRATCHY REALLY QUICKLY, PARTICULARLY IF YOU HAVE A COUPLE OF THEM. I'M JUST SAYING THEY'LL REACH AND POKE ANYWHERE AND THEY HAVE THOSE LONG SPINDLY FINGERS. A FIRM PUNCH TO THE HEAD WILL KNOCK MOST OF THEM UNCONSCIOUS BUT YOU GOTTA BE CAREFUL AS THEY CAN PRETEND TO BE DOWN WHEN THEY'RE REALLY TRYING TO USE THEIR MIND-CONTROL TRICKS ON YOU.

MEN IN BLACK REPORT (AGENT MIB 233), NEW YORK CITY

STEP 1
THE CRAZY APE

The best weapons you have against the Greys are brute strength and shock tactics. Choose your time to strike then move like a wild animal, punching and kicking in all directions. For kicks, it's best to aim low, to the stomach or back, where the Grey nervous system is most vulnerable. Maintain your anti-mind-probe defences as you swing and punch during your 'crazy ape' combat routine.

ALIEN COMBAT
AVOIDING MIND CONTROL

A telepathic attack is the first wave of assault for any Grey in combat. These aliens are capable of using their well-developed mind skills to 'get inside the head' of their opponent and avoid any physical combat before it even begins. Combat moves such as the 'crazy ape' outlined below can help you resist alien mind probes, for an enhanced level of rage and anger presents a natural barrier against an external force trying to take over your actions. However, you must supplement this to ensure that other nearby creatures can't implant their agenda when your 'anger barriers' are down. Use music if you can; 1980s pop seems to work well, particularly the music of Culture Club or the *Rocky* movies.

THE INSPIRATIONAL MUSIC FROM THE *ROCKY* MOVIES, PARTICULARLY *ROCKY IV*, HAS BEEN PROVEN TO HELP PREVENT ALIEN MIND CONTROL.

This kick is too low to duck – counter with block?

STEP 2
BEWARE OF THE SAUCER KICK

Although weaker than humans, Greys are very aware of human physiology and know our weak spots. They have no qualms about groin shots or eye pokes and their spindly limbs can be hard to pin down. Interestingly, the Greys seem to have developed some anti-human moves since 1980, including a flying kick known as the 'saucer kick' due to the fact that the alien can apparently spin in mid-air.

STEP 3
GOING 'GEORGE FOREMAN' ON ET

The most vulnerable points on a Grey are the skull and large black eyes. As with the rest of the body, the skull is made of flexible bone, but any Grey can be taken out with a well-placed punch. Their over-sized eyes and thin, transparent eyelids are an excellent target for any liquids or sharp objects. Practise your front jabs and punches regularly as part of your defence routine.

ALIEN COMBAT

COMBAT AGAINST LITTLE GREEN MEN

Although similar to Greys in that they're smaller and considerable weaker physically than an adult human, Little Green Men couldn't be more different in terms of their mentality. These aliens are bullies. They've been observed fighting among themselves in duels. When this happens, they strip down so they're just wearing their little trousers and start circling each other, hissing and screaming obvious insults and obscenities. A duel between Little Green Men was actually witnessed by a female Nigerian agent of the Men in Black in 2008 and she reported that it was like watching 'two angry garden gnomes going at each other'.

Little Green Men are vulnerable to any head shots as the skull has only a very thin bone cover. They're often seen wearing armour-like outfits and carrying all kinds of poison spray, darts and other unpleasant accessories. A clean bash to the top of the head will render a Little Green Man incapacitated for some time. He'll collapse on the floor, overcome by dizziness, and sometimes start singing in a high-pitched voice. It sounds funny but just remember that these are deadly creatures who'll take a pot shot at you with their ray guns whenever they can!

Little Green Men often make use of 'minions' such as brainwashed humans or enslaved alien species, so assume that any creature with them has been twisted to do their evil green bidding.

COMBAT AGAINST LITTLE GREEN MEN

LITTLE GREEN MEN AND MODERN WEAPONS

As with other alien species, much of the modern weaponry in the human arsenal is useless against the Little Green Men and this species has a long history of being able to create 'electronic interference' in any defence systems. For example, in one case they almost launched a nuclear missile from a Soviet site in the Ukraine. However, in combat the Little Green Men relish facing an armed opponent – particularly if you have a hand gun or similar. If you engage them with such a weapon, you can look forward to a Wild West-style shoot-out – a form of combat the Little Green Men relish. These creatures are largely untrustworthy and dishonourable so be cautious when engaging them.

> AN LGM WILL NEVER FIGHT UNARMED BUT IT'S RARE TO FIND ONE WITHOUT THAT SMALL RAY GUN THEY ALL CARRY. IF YOU KNOCK THAT OUT, THEY TEND TO MAKE A RUN FOR IT. THEY'RE SCARED TO FIGHT WITHOUT WEAPONS BUT WILL ALWAYS COME BACK. THEY ALSO LIKE TO HIDE AND IF TRAPPED WILL LEAP OUT TO ATTACK. IT'S WORTH REMEMBERING THAT THEY HAVE VERY SENSITIVE HEARING DESPITE ALL THE NOISE THEY MAKE, SO SHOUTING OR SINGING DOES SEEM TO DISTRACT THEM, PARTICULARLY IRRITATING BUBBLE GUM POP OR ANY HIGHLY REPETITIVE TUNE.
> **MEN IN BLACK REPORT (AGENT MIB 113), LAGOS, NIGERIA**

STEP 1
HIDE OR FLIGHT

Never face a Little Green Man head-on. They're always armed and are expert shots. Don't try to surrender as they're trigger-happy and always ready to vaporise an alien. If possible, either get away or conceal yourself from their view. Little Green Men have relatively poor eyesight: if you're caught in the open, freeze and wait for them to pass. They're unlikely to spot you as long as you don't move.

⚠️ ALIEN COMBAT
THE CLASSIC RAY GUN

Little Green Men and many other alien species use directed-energy weapons or 'ray guns'. In fact, it's now thought that many of the ray guns seen in science fiction are based on sketches of the actual weapons found at LGM crash sites. For the LGMs, ray guns are almost a way of life. These aliens are almost always seen carrying a ray gun and pride themselves on their accuracy with the weapon. There's known to be a rifle variant but for the most part LGMs seem to prefer to carry a smaller gun, or even two of them. The ray gun is considered a status symbol in their society and losing it or being disarmed is a shameful experience for an LGM. In fact, from the little experience we have of combat with LGMs, it has been observed that if they feel threatened or are caught by surprise, these aliens would rather make a run for it and keep their weapons.

STEP 2
DISARM YOUR OPPONENT

If you're forced into combat with a Little Green Man, it's essential that you separate the alien from its ray gun. The most effective way to do this is by using a rock or stone and throwing it hard towards the creature. A Little Green Man tends to panic without its gun and it will immediately look around trying to find the weapon. If the alien is unable to recover its ray gun, it may well turn tail and run away.

STEP 3
THE 'YAK, YAK, YAK' ATTACK!

The best attack move is to run towards the alien screaming 'Yak, Yak, Yak!' at the top of your voice. Uttering 'Yak' three times is considered blasphemy by the Little Green Men. Keep on screaming as you close in and, once you're within reach, deliver a wide clapping movement so that a hand smacks either side of your opponent's green head. You can also hammer two fists repeatedly on top of the head.

ALIEN COMBAT

COMBAT AGAINST DRACONIANS

By nature, Draconians are a non-violent species. They look upon physical combat as beneath them. We know, for example, that they attend school as hatchlings for over 100 Earth years and that for much of this time they're taught politics and are thus expert at manipulation and clever word play.

Deception is a highly prized quality among Draconians and is admired as courage is in humans. However, it's worth noting that when directly confronted Draconians can and will use violence. They tend to be clumsy and heavy-handed fighters, swinging their large arms and using a style of combat akin to wrestling. They've been known to change shape, colour and form when fighting.

Draconians don't function well in colder temperatures, with some experts suggesting that anything below 18°C impacts on their ability to react in combat. So, if you do suspect a 'human' of being a shape-shifting Draconian, try turning up the air conditioning and noting any reaction.

Draconians are vulnerable to particular matter in the air – so dust or any aerosol spray is unpleasant for them and sometimes makes it difficult for them to breath. As you can imagine, older air conditioning units – with their polluted and dusty output – can be extremely useful.

It's difficult for Draconians to last for more than eight hours without sustenance and they become prone to lapses in energy when this occurs.

► COMBAT AGAINST DRACONIANS

WEAPONS AGAINST THE LIZARDS

The Draconians so far seen on Earth have a hard, scaly skin that's resistant to most weapons. There are no recorded incidents of firearms being used on a lizard but current thinking is that pistols and shotguns may struggle to make much impact, although high-velocity weapons would be effective. Key Draconian organs are set deep within the body and our intelligence suggests that the creatures can easily function with arms or legs missing – and can even grow them back given time. It's important to note that the guidance given here still applies when facing a shape-shifted Draconian; if, for example, a lizard shape-shifts into human form, behind the altered external appearance the inside of the creature will remain 100% reptile.

> THE DRACONIANS ARE BIG, POWERFUL ALIENS AND, ONCE RILED, THEY'RE HARD TO CALM DOWN. MOST STAND TALLER THAN HUMANS AND YOU GOTTA WATCH THAT SPITTLE AS IT STINGS LIKE ANYTHING AND CAN BLIND IF THEY GET YOU IN THE EYES. PHYSICALLY, IT'S HARD TO TAKE THEM ON. THEY HAVE A LOW CENTRE OF GRAVITY AND THOSE CLAWS ARE PAINFUL. BEST POLICY IS TO STAMP ON THE TAIL, IF THEY HAVE ONE. THEY'RE REALLY SENSITIVE TO ANY AIR POLLUTANTS SUCH AS DEODORANT SPRAYS.
>
> MEN IN BLACK REPORT (AGENT MIB 712), TOKYO, JAPAN

STEP 1
THE SHAPE-SHIFT SHUFFLE

If you spot a shimmering halo around someone, it's quite possible that they're shape-shifting back into their true form. In alien combat, this is known as the 'shape-shift shuffle' and the creature is vulnerable for a few seconds as it changes. Grab any weapon you can and strike if you have the time. If not, this is your chance to run for it.

ALIEN COMBAT
ALIEN-FU ON THE MOVE

Stock up on deodorant – lizards don't like it in the face plus you never know when you might meet someone new

It's impossible to cover every scenario in this short survey of Alien-Fu techniques but there are whole sections designed to help you stay safe on the move. Alien-Fu is far more than just a martial art – it's a state of mind. It's about staying safe when the world around is going crazy.

- Find a hiding place – think low, dark and damp. All of this can interfere with sensors. Basements, tunnels, drains.
- Stay calm – rapid breathing and heartbeat will make detection easier for alien sensors.
- Merge in with other life forms – if you're caught in the open, hide among trees, foliage, even a herd of cows. Aliens aren't always sure what a human looks like.

- If you have no other option, dig a shallow hole and line the bottom with foil, then lie down with foil on top of you.
- Don't use any transmitting devices. Any mobile phones, radios or even MP3 players could lead the aliens to you.
- As a general rule, wait at least an hour until you emerge once the noise of the aliens has gone.
- Submerging in water may confuse some species as they may strictly adhere to the rule that humans need oxygen.

YOU WON'T ALWAYS BE ABLE TO FIGHT – THERE MAY BE TIMES WHEN YOU SIMPLY NEED TO HIDE TO SURVIVE.

STEP 2
ACID SPRAY!

When a Draconian shape-shifts back into lizard form and senses any danger, it instinctively spits acidic bile that can travel up to 10 metres. You should quickly drop to one knee to avoid this painful acid. If you don't have time or can't duck, then hold up a bag or similar to protect your face. If the bile gets on your skin, wash immediately with cold water.

This old girl can really move – she could follow up with a handbag whack

STEP 3
THE TAIL STAMP

Most humans wouldn't last long in a straight punching fight with a Draconian, but these aliens have vulnerabilities. Stamping your heel hard on the end of the tail can cripple a Draconian as this area is a nerve hub and such a blow is very painful for them. Equally, firing pepper spray into their faces can leave the lizards coughing and heaving up.

COMBAT AGAINST INSECTOIDS

As far as we know, no human has ever faced an Insectoid in combat. We have very limited knowledge of their ships, weapons and the soldier drones who would be expected to do most of the fighting should this species decide to invade Earth. We rely heavily on information given to humanity during our dialogue with the Greys: while we have no reason to question this data, some observers have noted that even the Greys themselves only seem to have second-hand knowledge of the species. Even in a universe as big as ours, the Insectoids are a species that most aliens just want to stay away from.

In 2010, the Massachusetts Institute of Technology ran a six-week war game simulation using their powerful RADX computer system. The scenario looked at an Insectoid invasion of Earth from a single hive ship. It assumed that any attack directed at the alien vessel in space had failed and that humanity was facing a war against billions of soldier drones fired down to the surface from the orbiting hive ship. The scenario was run ten times during the allotted timeframe and on each occasion humanity faced complete extinction within six to eight weeks.

One outcome of this study was that the US military commissioned an assessment of the potential use as a weapon of the fungus *Ophiocordyceps Unilateralis*. We may yet be able to use this fungus, which attacks ants in Asian jungles, to destroy any Insectoid invaders.

▶ COMBAT AGAINST INSECTOIDS

BUGS AND FIREARMS

Insectoid soldiers are fast-moving, spindly creatures that present a difficult target when using firearms. Current orthodoxy is to aim for the black 'skull' of the creature or, failing that, the central body or thorax. We know that soldiers are extremely robust and can continue to function if a limb is removed – so don't assume that a creature is out of action because it's down. Compound eyes are obvious targets on every Insectoid but firearms experts suggest that the creature's angled eyes may have been designed to deflect projectiles. Experts have also concluded that weapons such as shotguns and most handguns are unable to cause significant injury to an Insectoid soldier.

> ❝ NO HUMAN CAN GIVE YOU A FULL RUN-DOWN ON THIS ENEMY. THERE'S A LOT OF MATERIAL OUT THERE ON THE WEB BUT TO THE BEST OF OUR KNOWLEDGE NONE OF IT IS ACTUALLY FIRST-HAND. THERE'S A LOT OF THEORY, A LOT OF CONJECTURE AND A LOT THAT'S BEEN MADE UP. THE BEST ADVICE WE CAN GIVE CADETS IS TO READ UP THOROUGHLY ON INSECT BEHAVIOUR HERE ON EARTH. WE KNOW THE HIVE HAS HUNDREDS OF THOUSANDS OF YEARS OF EVOLUTION OVER THE INSECT SPECIES HERE, BUT MAYBE WE CAN FIND SOMETHING TO OUR ADVANTAGE. ❞

MEN IN BLACK REPORT (AGENT MIB 998), TRAINING CAMP

STEP 1
MANDIBLE MASH-UP

The soldier drones' primary method of combat is physical – using their large jaws or mandibles to cut through the flesh or armour of opponents. They may also be armed with acidic sprays or gases. Only attack these creatures from a safe distance as humans have no chance in hand-to-hand combat. If you have no other alternative, press your thumbs into their compound eyes or try to pull off their antennae.

ALIEN COMBAT
THE INSECTOID–DRACONIAN WAR

The hive is arranged along polymorphic lines, meaning that different physical castes have been developed. It's believed that there are types of soldier drone with the ability to adapt to different opponents.

According to the Greys, the Draconians fought a long, hard and devastating war against the hive during which the Insectoids fielded soldier drones capable of firing or injecting chemical poisons. It's believed that the hive is able to change the composition of these toxins according to the nature of the enemy. Another type of soldier drone fires tiny shards of hard, bone-like material.

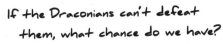

If the Draconians can't defeat them, what chance do we have?

STEP 2
A SWARM

The most important thing to remember about Insectoid soldier drones is that their strength is in their numbers. Drones typically overcome an opponent by simply over-running them, so avoid open spaces where Insectoids can use their numbers to their advantage. A single drone, however, can be defeated: a bullet to the alitrunk – the body's central part – will incapacitate a drone.

STEP 3
AIM FOR THE ANTENNAE

If you find yourself facing a soldier drone, the best weapon (if you don't have a firearm) would be something long and heavy such as a stout broom. Think of it as a sweeping weapon that will enable you to stay out of reach of the creature. A good strike at the antennal fossa (where the antennae meet the 'skull') is the best target. This could leave the creature disorientated and unbalanced.

ALIEN COMBAT

ESCAPING FROM A HOLDING CELL

If, for whatever reason, you find yourself imprisoned on an alien craft, you must decide your course of action extremely carefully.

Although any alien invader will have carried out extensive studies of the human race and acquired in-depth knowledge of our biological requirements, it's surprising how often their holding cells are basic and not necessarily impregnable. Aliens, it seems, tend to underestimate the adaptability and cunning of humans, despite their considerable intellectual superiority over us. Logic would suggest that any alien able to perform mental arithmetic to 200 decimal places with absolute ease ought to have the common-sense to construct holding cells that are escape-proof!

OUR ADVANTAGE

Whether you're held in an examination room after abduction or have been captured during full-scale invasion, alien species in general will under-estimate you in two main respects:

▶ The human spirit and belief that you can survive. We're a species that doesn't give up easily. We'll continue fighting and, at our best, we're capable of great feats and heroism.
▶ The deviousness and craftiness of humanity. Our ability to lie or tell half-truths is a challenging concept to most species, particularly the Greys. Most aliens are aware of this particular 'talent' of ours, so in your answers keep things 'blurred' – merge lies with truth and mix up logic to confuse them as much as possible.

▶ OPTIONS FOR ESCAPE

Your first action if you find yourself locked in an alien holding cell is to make a thorough assessment of the area. Pay particular attention to the doors, any windows and ventilation. If you're sharing the cell with other prisoners, keep your observations to yourself, at least initially.

Be cautious of other captives. If they're humans, look for proof that they're not clones – try to get a look at the belly-button area and quiz them with quick-fire questions about Earth. Although most clones are able to access a human memory, it isn't always easy for them to do so quickly or efficiently.

OPTION 1
DOORS

Doors provide the most obvious escape opportunities. Check any electronic panels by the door sides. Look for any way in which you might be able to 'short circuit' the mechanism. Also check for any magnetic seal at the bottom of the door. In some cases, just breaking this circuit will cause the door to slide open. Remember, these doors weren't designed to keep humans in.

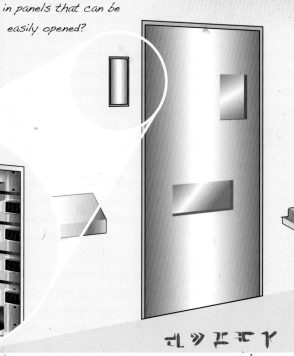

Why do aliens build delicate circuitry in panels that can be easily opened?

- Our sheer aggressiveness. Clearly there's some irony in the fact that an alien species invading Earth finds humanity aggressive, but this trait is more to do with our physical aggressiveness and scheming rather than any ruthlessness on a strategic level. We're often seen as an unpredictable and confusing species to aliens. Think of this: with our size, smell and irrationality, an angry, violent human seems much the same to species such as the Greys and the Little Green Men as a rampaging, out-of-control ape would seem to to us – powerful, scary, unpredictable and not particularly bright.
- Remember that most aliens find our species pretty repulsive and germ-ridden. In general, they'll want to keep away from our blood, saliva or any other bodily fluid. If you're suffering from a cold or, better still, the flu, then ensure that you wipe your infected hands along every wall and across every door whenever you can.

ADAPT YOUR PLAN

As a final observation, take into account that alien species aren't all the same. What shocks the Greys may be nothing to the more worldly Draconians. When in groups, Little Green Men can behave very aggressively and with child-like tantrums. Always adapt your plans according to your opponent. Know them and their weaknesses, as explored in earlier chapters.

DRACONIANS MAY HAVE A MORE IN-DEPTH UNDERSTANDING OF HUMAN NATURE BUT THEY STILL FIND ACTIONS SUCH AS COVERT HUMMING INCREDIBLY IRRITATING. AN INEXPERIENCED DRACONIAN COULD SPEND HOURS SEARCHING FOR THE NOISE, WITH EACH HUMAN DECLARING IN TURN THAT IT ISN'T THEM – AND YET THE HUMMING PERSISTS. THIS TACTIC CAN BE USED TO CONFUSE OR DISTRACT.

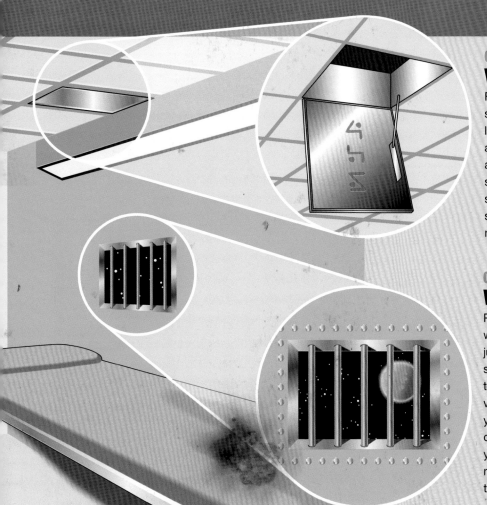

OPTION 2
VENTILATION SHAFT

Frequently guarded by only a poorly screwed-in grille, shafts are typically large enough for a human to crawl into and often lead easily to other parts of a ship. In reality we know that most smaller craft lack any large ventilation shaft, but larger ships invariably have a system of shafts that can be used for making your escape.

OPTION 3
WINDOWS

Prison cells on space ships rarely have windows and, if they do, the view usually just shows the endless blackness of space. However, windows can be useful to help you get your bearings. On most vessels you won't know whether or not you're moving due to the sophistication of the internal gravity systems – but if you can see a planet or even Earth you may be able adapt your escape plans to take this into account.

ALIEN COMBAT

ESCAPE SCENARIOS

Learning how to escape from an alien holding cell is an invaluable skill, but once you've got that cold, metallic door open, you need to have a plan. Remember, if you find yourself trapped in an alien base or space craft, it's only a matter time before the aliens discover that you've escaped, so this section details four useful escape scenarios you can use should you find yourself held captive on an alien vessel. As you'll see, they range from freefalling through the upper atmosphere to paying the ultimate price for humanity and setting the alien self-destruct sequence with little or no hope for yourself. Whether you find yourself taken against your will by a wandering Grey saucer or captured by a Draconian invader intent on taking on the Earth, it's your duty as a human to escape and cause as much mayhem and chaos as possible for our alien enemies.

1 FREEFALLING FROM AN ALIEN SHIP

So, you've managed to escape your alien captors and several Greys lie knocked out on the silver floor. You've searched for an escape pod but can't find one. You find the exit hatch and remember how they operated it. You open it... you're more than 30,000 feet in the air, heading into space... your only chance is to jump for it!

Look around for any detachable door or sheet that you can use to 'fly down'. This is known as wreckage riding. It may be an object you can use to slow your descent or even something you can hide in and use for protection on landing. Know your physics. If you're falling towards Earth, its gravity will be pulling you downwards, so any drag you can create will restrict your level of acceleration towards terminal velocity! If you're jumping from a significant height, air will be an issue. Ensure that you take several deep breaths before you take the plunge.

Check if I can get a parachute into my daily bug-out bag

2 USING AN ALIEN TELEPORTER

We know less about the transportation beams used by aliens than perhaps any other area of ET technology. We simply don't currently have the physics to grasp how matter is broken down, transferred and then reassembled. We assume that the various species are using similar technology but to date humanity's only success has been some limited trials in Area 51 in which a One Direction DVD was dematerialised. Unfortunately (or fortunately) the scientists were unable to make it reappear again. Our official guideline would be to discourage usage of such technology as there are simply too many variables: the rematerialisation coordinates must be carefully set and then tested in some way or else you could end up reappearing halfway into the ground. You may be able to threaten an alien hostage to help you escape.

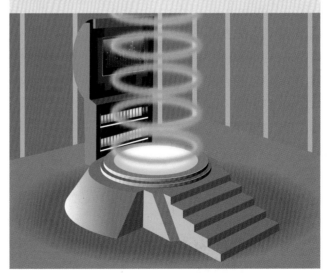

3 USING AN ALIEN ESCAPE POD

From the alien ships we have grounded on Earth, we can confirm that all of them have some kind of escape pod. This seems to be one area where the science-fiction writers got it right. To date, no escape pod has been successfully activated but this may be due to the fact that the craft are either damaged or already on the ground. What we've learned is that there are two clear types of escape pod – those that can be used at any time and those that require the ship to be at risk before being activated. In the case of the latter, once you've escaped you'll soon be able to put the ship 'at risk' by tripping alarms, and it's always worth pulling out a few bio-cables wherever you can find them. Cause as much chaos as possible as you make your way to an escape pod.

Most escape pods are brought online via a central control panel, then launched from within – so it may not always be possible to activate them. Take a few minutes, but if you can't figure it out just get moving – there'll be no time to waste. Lastly on escape pods, we have to be honest: there has never been a successful and documented human escape from an alien ship.

IN MOST VESSELS ESCAPE PODS ARE SITUATED ON THE LOWEST POINT OF THE SHIP AND AWAY FROM THE ENGINES. THERE'S LITTLE COLOUR ON A GREY SAUCER, EVERYTHING BEING A DULL SHADE OF GREY OR SILVER, BUT THE ESCAPE PODS HAVE RED MARKERS ON THEM. CHECKING THE SLIDING DOORS FOR THE RED MARKER IS A GOOD PLACE TO START.

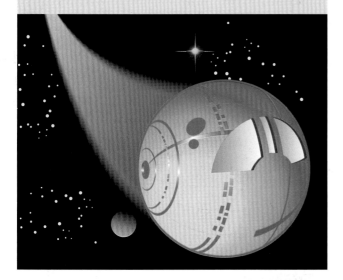

4 FINDING THE SELF-DESTRUCT BUTTON

Some of the guidance relating to teleportation applies equally to using a ship's auto-destruct sequence. We suspect that every ship has one but the chances of an untrained human being able to activate it would be slim. For sure, we know it won't be a big red button you can simply press to start a countdown. So, what are your other options if you decide you want to make the aliens really pay? The best policy is to head for the engine room. The black triangle ships of the Little Green Men use an anti-matter drive: meddle with this baby in their home system and you could end up unleashing a whole new black hole of pain for the green chaps. Wrecking a craft's propulsion system is the next best thing.

⚠ HOPE FOR THE BEST!

Escape may not always be possible, or you tried and were simply thrown back into your cell. The ship you're in is clearly en route somewhere – perhaps to dock with a mother ship or return to a home world or base. The balancing factor here is the aliens' intention: are you being taken back as part of an experiment, do they want to top up their supply of slaves, or might you become an inter-galactic delicacy to be served at some Jabba the Hutt-style feast? Most of the time you just won't know, so keep your eyes and ears open, and be ready to act if things get desperate.

GUIDELINES FOR MILITARY FORCES

Over a period of 12 months, some of the world's most sophisticated military simulation software ran thousands of invasion scenarios after being populated with every possible variable. The key findings offer some glimmer of hope that we can survive.

When military planners consider scenarios beyond their current frame of reference or with no historical precedent – such as a major planetary invasion of Earth – they turn to complex algorithms to help us consider factors that are essentially unknowns, such as the number of humans who will become turncoats and join the alien invaders or the impact of our weaponry on energy shields.

General Wang Li-Cha of the Chinese Red Army's Specialist Intelligence Division is a leading authority on alien invasion scenario analysis. The good news is that despite all of the technological advantages of an alien invader, General Li-Cha believes that we have a chance to successfully defend our world.

MOST ALIEN INVASION SCENARIOS SEE OUR PLANET DEVASTATED, WITH CASUALTIES INTO THE BILLIONS. HOWEVER, IF HISTORY HAS SHOWN US ANYTHING, IT IS THAT THE 'WEAK' CAN OVERCOME THE 'STRONG'.

PREPARATION

▶ With the right preparation, humanity can defeat a more technologically advanced opponent, but can expect huge numbers of casualties and planet-wide destruction.

▶ With major changes in our global level of preparation, we can massively improve our rates of survival. Top of the list of priorities are developing our space technology and working together as a species, so that humanity presents a unified and coordinated response worldwide.

▶ In some invasion scenarios, such as a war of extermination by Insectoids, there can be no 'Victory on Earth' outcome. As such, preparations should be made immediately for a Global Evacuation Initiative (GEI).

▶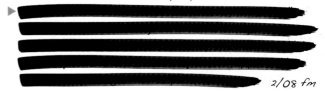

2/08 fm

GUIDELINES FOR MILITARY FORCES
THE SCIENTIFIC VIEW

At the 2010 Stockholm Annual Seminar 344 of the world's top scientists were asked whether they believed humanity could survive an invasion by a technologically superior alien opponent. They were asked to set aside personal beliefs concerning the existence or otherwise of alien life and base their assessment on their knowledge of invasive species on Earth.

5% EVICTION
Some species relocate to evade a new invader – humanity may head out into the stars.

6% LIFE ON THE MARGINS
Human life as we know it would be pushed to the very margins of our planet.

10% EVOLUTION
To co-exist with any alien invader, humanity may evolve as other species do.

25% HUMAN RESOURCES
An imperialist alien force would eradicate any human resistance then use humanity as either slave labour or a food supply.

54% EXTINCTION
Humanity would be superseded by an aggressive superior species and become extinct in line with natural law.

SURVEY BY U-POL, JUNE 2010, 344 RESPONDENTS

 **MINISTRY OF ALIEN DEFENCE**

LESSONS FROM OUR HISTORY

Biologists here on Earth have played a significant role in helping to build the invasion scenarios in this manual. For example, the theory of invasive species in nature is used to analyse how an 'alien' species invades a new eco-system – think of grey squirrels in the UK or red imported fire ants in the US. The model of invasive species outlines four key factors to consider. In the table below, we have taken these factors and overlaid them on to an alien invasion scenario.

SOURCE POPULATION	PATHWAYS
▶ The native eco-system: Earth and humanity	▶ Possible routes to the source population
▶ A large population of a humanoid species	▶ Invasion from orbit
▶ Limited technology	▶ Covert operations from Earth
▶ Tribal	▶ Dimensional attack
▶ Confident in its superiority	
▶ Unprepared for a species assault	

DESTINATION	VECTORS
▶ Earth (primary target), plus moon and solar system	▶ Means of following pathways
▶ Great bio-diversity on Earth	▶ Invasion via inter-galactic ships
▶ Limited resources on other planets	▶ Teleportation
	▶ Asteroid attack

WHAT THIS TELLS US

Laying this model over what we know about alien species is a frightening exercise and it becomes worse when you consider some of the ecological rules of species warfare seen so far on this planet. For example, the propensity is that the longer an invasive species stays and builds, the higher the chance of it establishing and superseding a native one. Therefore, it would seem that any alien invasion would need to be defeated quickly, if at all possible.

Another worrying 'rule' is that any invading species would need a new habitat to be compatible with their own requirements and preferences. We know that Little Green Men and the Draconians would want to adapt our planet's physical environment into a more suitable state for themselves if they intended to make Earth their own.

▶ ENERGY SHIELDS

Energy shields – also known as force fields, deflectors or plasma shields – are made up of 'energy' or particles and surround an object or individual, providing protection from hostile attacks. We know that most alien invaders would make use of such weapons. Scientists regard energy shields as a typical example of a 'species gap' – a technology in which the aliens are so far advanced that we face a significant challenge overcoming it. If there are too many of these 'gaps', humanity will be toast when the aliens invade.

Here's a quick summary of what we currently know about alien energy shields.

WHO HAS THEM?

Every advanced alien species uses energy shields on their spacecraft to protect them from destruction by even the smallest of obstacles – essential for inter-stellar space travel. Energy shields give aliens a massive tactical advantage over humanity, particularly in air combat. It would be extremely difficult, perhaps impossible, for humanity to shoot down a fully shielded alien ship.

DO WE UNDERSTAND THEM?

The Americans have had some limited success in understanding energy shields when reverse-engineering a crashed Grey saucer in Area 51. In 1973 the shields automatically flicked on for a period of four days shortly after a scientist working nearby opened a packet of crisps – the flavour was cheese and onion. After the shields shut down again it proved impossible to reactivate them, but the team at Area 51 did gain some insight into the protection an energy shield provides. If you spot an alien vessel on the ground, it's worth observing how aliens move through a shielded area – are the shields dropped to allow exit and entry?

ALIEN ENERGY SHIELDS DEFEND THE VESSEL FROM ANY PROJECTILE WEAPONS. NO MISSILES, BULLETS OR EXPLOSIVES THAT WE CURRENTLY POSSESS CAN GET THROUGH A FULLY CHARGED ENERGY SHIELD. OCCASIONALLY, DAMAGED SHIPS CAN DEVELOP A FAINT FLICKER IN THEIR SHIELDS; THIS MAY PRESENT A VERY SMALL WINDOW OF OPPORTUNITY TO ASSAULT THE VESSEL.

ALIEN VIEWS OF HUMANITY

Before profiling any invasion scenarios, it's worth considering how potential invaders may view humanity and our capacity to defend the planet. So far, we've examined technological levels, military capabilities and drivers for the various species, but to really know our enemy we need some insight into how they view us.

Here at the Ministry of Alien Defence in London, we recently purchased a 16k RAM pack for our ZX81 computer and ran some analysis to try to ascertain how an 'alien mind' might view humanity. Admittedly, it did take a while but after several crashes we managed to extract the data on a tiny roll printer.

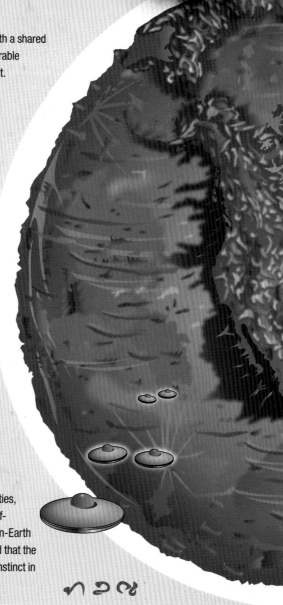

▶ HUMANITY'S WEAKNESSES

1 A DIVIDED PLANET

Humanity is divided into numerous groups and sub-groups. It has never been a unified entity with a shared command and control centre and any alliances could split in extreme adversity. There's considerable tension among humans along the lines of race and religion that could be exploited during conflict.

2 A LOW LEVEL OF TECHNOLOGY

Humanity has yet to develop key technologies such as energy-efficient propulsion and inter-stellar space travel. Their systems and networks are extremely vulnerable to an attack from orbit and they have no defence infrastructure for their solar system. Their space reach extends as far as their local moon, where there isn't a permanent human presence; in addition, automated probes have landed on Earth's nearest planetary neighbour.

3 WEAK MILITARY CAPABILITY

Based on a low level of technological achievement, humanity is equipped with relatively weak and fragmented armed forces. They're divided along group lines, with poor contact and coordination between these major units. There's a reliance on basic projectile weapons and rudimentary nuclear weapons. They have no working energy weaponry or shield technology beyond metallic armour. They're increasingly using first-generation computer systems to support their military on simple and exposed networks.

4 BIOLOGICAL VULNERABILITY

Earth humanoids are vulnerable to slight temperature variations. They require regular liquid and sustenance intake. Their performance can drastically drop if either of these areas is compromised. Biologically, they're particularly vulnerable to viruses and to infections around their breathing mechanism. They also have an extremely inefficient reproduction cycle that leaves them incapable of replacing lost forces during combat within a reasonable timescale.

5 POOR INTELLIGENCE ON THE UNIVERSE

With little knowledge beyond their own system, Earth humanoids are over-confident in their abilities, with much of the populace dismissing any thought of an invasion by another species. They're self-obsessed and have few immediate plans to learn more about the universe. Their contact with non-Earth species is limited and they currently have no active galactic alliances, although it should be noted that the species of inter-dimensional travellers they refer to as the Nordics have shown a slight paternal instinct in dealings with the humans.

ANALYSING THE RESULTS

We have aggregated the analysis into the list of human weaknesses presented below. This assessment helps us to see how humanity is likely to be viewed from an alien's perspective, although individual species will judge us in their own different ways

This is a bit like getting a poor report at school – it makes grim but all-too-familiar reading. The two key areas where there's most room for improvement are clearly world unity and our deficiencies in space technology. Most aliens will easily see our weaknesses and will work to exploit them in any invasion, with our computer networks being particularly vulnerable to highly sophisticated cyber attacks.

But let's not get too depressed: aliens would also undertake a similar study of our relative strengths as part of their military assessment. So, we fired up the ZX81 again and came up with a list of human strengths.

ET will get some dangerous bio-diversity when I get hold of him...

HUMANITY'S STRENGTHS

1 ADAPTABILITY

The Earth humanoids are the most successful species on their planet and have been further strengthened by the intense rivalry between groups. Humans have at times performed incredible feats and now populate most parts of the planet's surface. They've shown they can survive 'off-world' and there's every reason to think that they could make use of any advanced technology if they are able to seize it.

2 CREATIVITY

Humans place great value on artistic endeavours and problem-solving. They have a keen if rudimentary interest in mathematics but have advanced significantly in recent decades. There are some individual humans who are now beginning to unravel a unified theory of universe creation. Combining adaptability and creativity could make them unpredictable opponents.

3 AGGRESSION

Competition for survival on their planet has typically been fierce, with the strongest of their species surviving. Humans are a war-like species at heart and have engaged in major and cruel conflicts across their planet, involving attacks on every member of an opposing tribe, including non-fighting humans. Occasionally, if motivated by a notion of 'the greater good', humans have been known to drive home attacks that directly lead to their own destruction. Many humans are also physically superior, being able to easily defeat many slightly built species in the universe in terms of strength and agility.

4 DANGEROUS BIO-DIVERSITY

Their home planet has an incredible complex eco-system with literally millions of types of life forms. Humanity has developed within this eco-system and is infected with thousands of symbiotic life forms that could be lethal to other species. In humanity's recent history, millions of other life forms have been wiped out by bacterial or viral infections, but humans seem to be able to recover from many of these infections after their hundreds of thousands of years of evolution on the planet. The planet's eco-system could be lethal to many galactic life forms: a recent Galactic Medical Convention voted Earth the most likely source of an 'end of the universe' virus.

5 QUICK LEARNERS

Humanity is advancing at such a rapid pace now that within 100 Earth years it can be expected to become a regional power in its quadrant of the galaxy. They went from their first powered flight to a moon landing in only 66 of their Earth cycles. They're on the cusp of making advances in faster-than-light travel, artificial intelligence and cryogenics.

GUIDELINES FOR MILITARY FORCES

FULL-SCALE PLANETARY ASSAULT

Frustrated by lack of cooperation with humans and against a background of abductions having provided insufficient biological material for their needs, the Greys assessed Earth invasion. Observing humanity's rapid progress in space technology, they may decide to act.

A full-scale planetary assault would come in many forms, including bombardment from orbit or a surprise 'Pearl Harbour' attack on vital infrastructure and military forces. Overwhelming force would be used to eradicate any air power. This would be followed by a limited ground assault as the Greys could achieve their objectives by using huge ships to collect the bio-matter they require.

► MOTIVATION

The very survival of their species. With the failure of their policy of cooperation and abduction, the Greys will switch to a planet-wide programme to collect vast quantities of bio-matter from Earth, including humanoids. They intend to study all biological material on the planet in the quest to address their cloning difficulties.

► CAPACITY TO WAGE WAR

We know that the Greys are equipped with a sizable fleet of flying saucers as well as hundreds of 'mother ship' saucers. Their energy shields make then impervious to most human weapons, including nuclear devices.

► STRATEGY AND TACTICS

Grey intelligence informs us that when the decision is made to take military action, the species will opt to use overwhelming force in a coordinated attack.

► ALIEN RESILIENCE

Although the Greys have the resources from several planetary systems that they already dominate, it's believed that they see the rich bio-diversity of Earth as their 'salvation' and their need for it is increasingly urgent. Greys are very sensitive to suffering casualities and will most likely try to fight their war from a safe distance. Expect drones, mother ships and air bombardment.

 ### SCENARIO DEBRIEF

An invasion by Grey aliens would be a classic military invasion with strong echoes of tactics that human forces have used on Earth, such as the Blitzkrieg by Nazi Germany in 1939–42 and, more recently, the allied destruction of Iraqi forces in the early 1990s.

Our satellite and communication networks are extremely vulnerable to alien attack and our defensive software technology is rudimentary compared to what other species have developed. Our air power and infrastructure would be systematically taken out by the Greys' forces.

Humanity's capability to defend itself would be reduced, freeing the skies for the Greys to begin their exploitation plans unhindered by any organised resistance.

If Earth forces faced such a technologically advanced opponent head-on, they would be destroyed. It's vital, therefore, to focus our tactics and resources on key areas where we can disrupt and hamper the enemy's plans.

Military forces should avoid an open-air war with the Greys as their Type 1 saucers would tear any human forces to shreds.

▶ GREY INVASION TIMELINE • SCENARIO 121212/HH

1980
COLLAPSE OF THE TREATY OF GREADA

▶ The Greys' relationship with humanity finally breaks down and the aliens officially leave Earth. There's now no formal agreement between the Greys and humanity. The central Grey command structure makes the decision that they will take by force what they cannot obtain by peaceful means.

1990s
AIRSPACE VIOLATIONS BY GREY SAUCERS

▶ The Greys continue to take humans by force for their DNA experiments but they're now free to use whatever means and methods they see fit. There's an increase in the number of unreturned abductees. More aggressive scouting and intelligence is carried out by Grey saucers. Invasion plans are prepared.

CONTACT
A GIANT GREY SAUCER ENTERS OUR SOLAR SYSTEM

▶ A Grey saucer of exceptional size is seen for the first time and many observers suspect the presence of a new species. Attempts at contact fail and humanity has no military equipment capable of intercepting such a vessel.

▶ Newspapers and TV reports cover the story. There are outbreaks of violence and some cults insist it's the end of the world – but our military forces do nothing. The UN emphasises that the aliens may be friendly.

CONTACT +3 DAYS
GREY SAUCER ENTERS EARTH ORBIT

▶ There's still no response from the giant ship. Shortly after it enters Earth's orbit, smaller Grey saucers break away from the mother ship and head into Earth's atmosphere. These smaller saucers are still of enormous size – two miles in diameter.

CONTACT +4 DAYS
MOVING INTO STRIKE POSITIONS

▶ There's chaos on Earth as these two-mile saucers take up strategic positions over major cities. Military experts insist this is a strike pattern but politicians are reluctant to make the first aggressive move.

▶ A mysterious software virus takes out every Earth satellite and paralyses communication networks.

CONTACT +5 DAYS
D-DAY

▶ The alien saucers launch energy weapon strikes on every major city, destroying command structures and communication hubs. Smaller saucers break off and complete missions on many targets, including military sites.

▶ Humanity scrambles its military forces, but jet fighters are swept from the skies, unable to penetrate the energy shielding of the Greys' ships.

CONTACT +8 DAYS
AIR SUPERIORITY

▶ Through days of continuous strikes, the Greys' invasion forces have secured complete air superiority over Earth. All major military concentrations have been decimated and the command and control systems have been destroyed.

▶ The Greys have yet to set foot on the planet during this phase but sporadic attacks continue on infrastructure sites. These assaults are designed to hasten the collapse of organised human resistance rather than to kill millions.

CONTACT +30 DAYS
PACIFICATION

▶ Humanity suffers weeks of sustained bombardment and harassment. The last vestiges of organised government are sought out and destroyed. The Greys introduce new energy weapons that are capable of reaching deep, protected concrete bunkers. Adapted Type 1 saucers patrol the skies, monitoring any remaining transmissions by humanity.

CONTACT +40 DAYS
THE BIO-MATTER COLLECTORS

▶ A new type of ship appears in the skies over Earth. Thousands of large block-shaped craft appear and take up positions about 500 metres above Earth's surface. These are the Greys' bio-matter collectors. Once stationed, these vessels set off along programmed paths, using powerful tractor beams to pull up all bio-matter into their vast hulls. The bio-matter is quickly processed within and waste material ejected from the rear of the vessels.

CONTACT +30 YEARS
THE DEAD PLANET

▶ A few million humans remain, mainly in the mountainous regions, eking out a living from what they can find while the bio-matter ships continue their work. The great saucer in orbit left after 20 years, leaving a large space station in its place. This is the processing centre for all of the collected bio-matter. Life has been ripped from the Earth and vast tracts of the planet are now completely sterile.

STOPPING THE GREYS

Unlike other alien species, we've had direct experience of battling the Greys, at Dulce Airbase in 1980. From this we know that the Greys don't relish hand-to-hand combat. Despite the Greys having some advanced weapons and gadgets, a highly skilled team of US Special Forces managed to inflict high casualties on the aliens holding out at this secret base. So, don't expect to see Greys on the ground during an invasion. It's possible that they'll make use of tripods to seize particular high-value targets.

In a textbook Grey alien invasion, the visitors will never need to set foot on the planet. Their giant saucers and smaller fighting saucers will do the work for them.

▶ ATTACKING A BASE SHIP

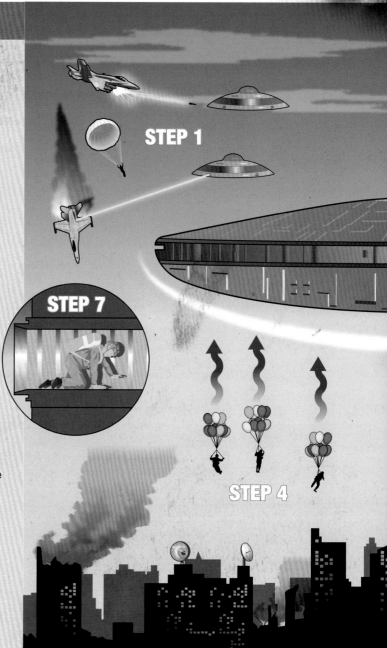

It's estimated that there will be hundreds of Type 1 saucers and these will be almost impossible for our military forces to shoot down due to their shielding. Therefore, our focus should be on the giant saucers and later the bio-collectors when they arrive.

BASE SHIPS WITHIN EARTH'S ATMOSPHERE

Attacking ships such as one of the larger Grey saucers would be a dangerous mission and one that would cost human lives. These giant vessels will typically be found hovering a mile or two above cities and will be well-defended for most attacks. This is why humanity should go back to basics.

Forget jets, missiles and any other modern weaponry – the Greys are high-tech operators and therefore we need to go low-tech to bring them down. This assault will be carried out by commandos in balloons and gliders. While the risks for these brave fighters will be high, the potential rewards for humanity will be immense.

If human forces can coordinate such attacks around the world, one can only imagine the impact a successful campaign would have on humanity and on the Greys themselves. Perhaps the Greys will deem the cost of their invasion too high, or perhaps they will be forced to evacuate a failing ship, offering us the chance to take hostages and give us significant advantage – the Greys, like the Little Green Men, are particularly susceptible to casualties.

THE TACTICS REVIEWED IN THIS SECTION MAY BE APPLIED TO ANY ALIEN VESSEL WITHIN EARTH'S ATMOSPHERE. THE LARGE GREY SAUCER IS THE MOST OBVIOUS EXAMPLE, BUT THE ATTACK STRATEGIES COULD APPLY TO ANY SHIELDED ALIEN SHIP.

THE STRATEGY FOR HUMANITY

To be clear, the Greys' objective is to eradicate any human resistance and then facilitate wholesale collection of Earth's biological material, including human beings. All human forces should stay away from a direct confrontation with Grey saucers. Key infrastructure sites should be evacuated or concealed and key military assets hidden. The strategy of humanity should be to avoid the hammer blow of the Grey assault, so forces should be split into smaller units and equipped with low-tech communications that will avoid the attention of our alien attackers – all military sites, for example, should be hooked up to telegraph wires.

Core texts to help prepare our military and civilian forces for this 'war' include the works of guerrilla leaders such as Mao Tse-Tung, particularly the 1947 second edition of his *Selected Military Writings* – a volume short on jokes but big on advice about how to defeat a more powerful opponent.

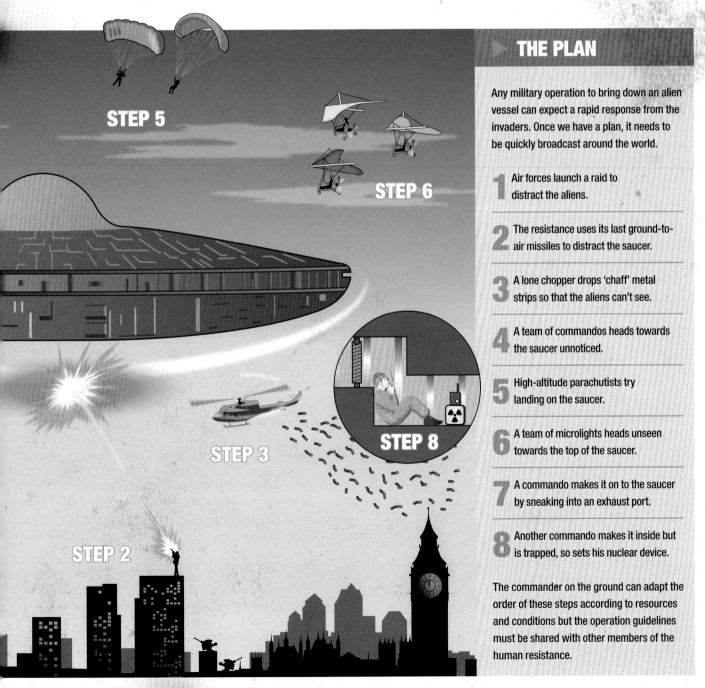

STEP 5

STEP 6

STEP 3

STEP 8

STEP 2

▶ THE PLAN

Any military operation to bring down an alien vessel can expect a rapid response from the invaders. Once we have a plan, it needs to be quickly broadcast around the world.

1 Air forces launch a raid to distract the aliens.

2 The resistance uses its last ground-to-air missiles to distract the saucer.

3 A lone chopper drops 'chaff' metal strips so that the aliens can't see.

4 A team of commandos heads towards the saucer unnoticed.

5 High-altitude parachutists try landing on the saucer.

6 A team of microlights heads unseen towards the top of the saucer.

7 A commando makes it on to the saucer by sneaking into an exhaust port.

8 Another commando makes it inside but is trapped, so sets his nuclear device.

The commander on the ground can adapt the order of these steps according to resources and conditions but the operation guidelines must be shared with other members of the human resistance.

LIMITED-SCALE PLANETARY ASSAULT

The Little Green Men (LGM) are an aggressive and ambitious race and growing Grey interest in Earth has only served to heighten their level of interest. Two factors – increased noise from this solar system and the emergence of human probes leaving the system – prompt these aliens to embark on an invasion of conquest.

A limited planetary assault is designed to crush human resistance without destroying the Earth or its potential. Most scenario planners see the destruction of a couple of cities as enough to terrorise the human population, followed by a ground assault designed to take over an already half-conquered people.

▶ MOTIVATION

The Little Green Men see Earth as a treasure trove of resources, including the use of humans as slave labour. Our planet would greatly extend their empire in this quadrant and give them a better base for expansion than their current bolthole on Mars. Their invasion would be with occupation very much in mind. They want to use the resources of Earth to serve their own needs.

▶ CAPACITY TO WAGE WAR

The Little Green Men have advanced triangle fighters as well as a hidden mother ship – although one has never been seen. It's most likely that they would operate from a major triangle ship in Earth's orbit, or even from Mars, where they have an old base.

▶ STRATEGY AND TACTICS

Humanity can expect a powerful assault from Earth orbit, possibly leading to the rapid destruction of one or two major population centres. The Little Green Men will seek to use overwhelming force, carefully targeted, to send a message to the world's population. They won't want to destroy any infrastructure that may be useful to their own needs. The ideal scenario for the Little Green Men may well be to work with a partner country on Earth – probably a minor 'rogue' one – and empower them to rule.

▶ ALIEN RESILIENCE

The Little Green Men are a proud species with no wish to be humiliated by an inferior one. With their technological advantage and their ruthlessness, they will destroy city after city if they have to until they get what they want – the submission of Earth. However, once they're in occupation, any Little Green Men on Earth and their 'forces of occupation' will be vulnerable. We know that the Little Green Men have a very hierarchical organisational structure with what Earth observers would call a 'blame culture'.

7/06
dst

 SCENARIO DEBRIEF

The objective of an invasion by Little Green Men would be total victory with as little effort as possible. Their experience has shown that a display of overwhelming force on a particular target can terrorise a population into submission. Thereafter they use a well-established strategy of finding human 'allies' to begin the systematic exploitation of the planet. In our scenario, the first planetary governor was removed as he didn't start to export resources quickly enough.

The Little Green Men don't expect to rule the Earth indefinitely. They'll be present just long enough to exploit every resource and then will depart, leaving Earth a broken planet.

▶ LITTLE GREEN MEN INVASION TIMELINE • SCENARIO 12132321/XY

UNKNOWN

THE CENTRAL LITTLE GREEN MEN COMMAND MAKES A DECISION TO INVADE EARTH

▶ It's currently believed that the Little Green Men are ruled by an emperor, although the individual is constantly changing due to infighting and complex patterns of politics and intrigue. It's therefore possible with a species such as the Little Green Men that no clear decision to invade will ever be made. However, they may deliberately engineer an incident or regard a crashed black triangle ship as an excuse for war.

UNKNOWN

THE LITTLE GREEN MEN RE-ESTABLISH A BASE ON MARS

▶ For many years the Little Green Men had a base on Mars that's thought to have served as a hub for various missions to Earth. Just prior to invasion it's expected that humans would notice many more 'black triangle incidents'. We have no information about the mother ship of the Little Green Men but we expect them to have large cruiser-type vessels.

CONTACT

THE LITTLE GREEN MEN ATTACK EARTH

▶ The Little Green Men launch unprovoked attacks on Tokyo and Cairo, destroying these two major cities. Local military forces attack the Little Green Men's fleet of ships but with no effect whatsoever, owing to their energy shields. Tens of millions are killed in this ruthless display of power.

CONTACT +3 DAYS

AN ULTIMATUM

▶ All previous attempts at communication from Earth to the invaders have failed but on the third day a simple message is sent to the United Nations in New York. It reads: 'Humans must bow down to their new masters now or face annihilation. One Earth day to respond.' National governments on Earth are thrown into chaos.

CONTACT +4 DAYS

BOLTS FROM THE SKY

▶ After allowing the impact of the destruction and ultimatum to sink in, the Little Green Men contact a 'rogue' state – North Korea – with an offer. They request a face-to-face meeting with the commanders of North Korea's military forces in order to secure their collaboration. The North Korean government agrees and soon the Little Green Men land on Earth for the first time since the invasion began and outline their demands for human support.

CONTACT +5 DAYS

NEW YORK AND BEIJING DESTROYED

▶ Black triangle ships strike again, wiping New York and Beijing from the face of the Earth. There are millions of casualties and many Earth governments are on the verge of collapse.

▶ Most world governments broadcast their surrender to the Little Green Men. A few defiant nations such as the UK vow to fight on. The Little Green Men order the surrendering governments to cut off these regions.

CONTACT +10 DAYS

PHONEY INVASION

▶ World governments are sent various instructions about providing detailed inventories of resources and assets. The Little Green Men demand that one human be in charge of each nation state. Any remaining military forces are to be used to keep law and order.

CONTACT +30 DAYS

OCCUPATION BEGINS

▶ After a period of relative quiet, the Little Green Men finally arrive in each national capital. They're accompanied by squads of North Korean guards in LGM-inspired uniforms and armed with a version of the LGM ray gun. Once immediate security is established, more Little Green Men arrive with tripods.

CONTACT +60 DAYS

THE WAR IS OVER

▶ The Little Green Men establish a governor in every major city and create a secret police led by their North Korean minions. Tripod-led punitive expeditions are directed against centres of resistance. The UK is pacified but resistance groups spring up in other parts of the world. An 'Emperor' takes overall control of Earth and sets up headquarters in the Vatican City. Humanity is divided.

CONTACT +120 DAYS

THE EXPLOITATION BEGINS

▶ A fleet of large freighters enters Earth orbit and the systematic exploitation of the planet begins. The first Little Green Men Emperor disappears and is replaced. The second is far more brutal, ordering that 100,000 humans be provided from every region. They must be fit and healthy and are destined for the galactic slave trade. An unusual ship is observed hovering over the Indian Ocean, drawing vast quantities of water from the planet.

GUIDELINES FOR MILITARY FORCES

STOPPING THE LITTLE GREEN MEN

We have no firm intelligence on specific Little Green Men invasion plans but with the information we have so far we can establish a *modus operandi* for these devious and dangerous creatures.

We know that their primary triangle ships are limited to around 0.9 light speed and therefore lack the capacity for inter-stellar travel. From study of wrecked triangle ships, we know that they're designed to dock on to a much larger 'mother ship'. There's probably only one such mother ship, as the Little Green Men are limited in number. We can assume that the mother ship is triangular in shape, although no human has ever seen one.

An invasion by the Little Green Men would see their mother ship enter our solar system, followed by a surprise attack of immense power on strategic targets. As the Little Green Men lack the numbers to sustain a planet-wide assault, a terrifying but limited display of their power is their most likely approach.

▶ ATTACKING AN ALIEN TRIPOD

Alien tripods have become the archetypical invasion weapon of choice in the minds of the general public since H.G. Wells's invaders used them to such great effect in his 1897 serialisation *War of the Worlds*. However, to the best of our knowledge it's only the Little Green Men who regularly use tripods, although the Greys also have them in their arsenal. So, as a general rule, if the Earth is facing an invasion by the Little Green Men then humanity will at some point face these awesome weapons in combat.

▶ Tripods are believed to come in three varieties: the lightweight patrol tripod, the heavy battle tripod (armoured with an energy shield) and the slightly larger, slower 'human scooper' variety equipped with extra arms, which are used to scoop up fleeing humans and place them in a large secure basket at the rear.

▶ Height is between 15 and 25 metres depending on model.

▶ Legs are made of an unknown metal alloy of dull grey colour that's highly resistant to projectile weapons.

▶ The patrol tripod can reach speeds of over 35mph, while the heavier battle and scooper tripods are believed to be capable of 20–25mph.

▶ Three large 'eyes' provide visual information to the cockpit, which contains three individuals – pilot, co-pilot and weapons operator.

▶ The primary weapon is a heavy-duty energy weapon that fires a concentrated laser beam. We don't know the range of the weapon but the battle experience of the Greys leads us to believe that it's effectively infinite when used on a planet's surface.

PLAN A
THREE-WAY RAM

The most direct form of attack is a three-way approach that targets the base of each leg simultaneously. The best delivery mechanism is to use heavy vans or trucks to ram the legs. The drawback of this plan is that the main ray gun is bound to take out at least one attacker unless timing is perfect, and the secondary ray guns can be expected to work on the other two attackers given a little time. The advantage of this plan is that only one attacker needs to make it through. It's worth timing the rams so that the attacker targeting the rear leg is the last to be spotted. A tripod is tail-heavy and an impact on the rear leg is the best way to bring one down.

 MINISTRY OF ALIEN DEFENCE

GUIDELINES FOR MILITARY FORCES
LITTLE GREEN MEN TRIPODS

Make a Michael Bolton mix tape – ideal music for tripod-busting

Tripods are used for multiple purposes, from front-line battle action to anti-resistance patrols. However, part of their purpose is to sow seeds of terror among the native population. The Little Green Men won't risk casualties to their own species and so prefer the protection of a machine to make up for their diminutive size. But they're also experts at spreading fear among their opponents and so their tripods have been designed to replicate some insect features; they know that the Insectoids are feared most of all.

The real question you should be asking as an ET prepper and human resistance fighter is this: 'How do I bring them down?' It's very unlikely that direct fire from human weapons will be able to bring down a tripod – they're well shielded from projectile weapons.

REMEMBER, THE THREE VISION EYES ARE THE MOST WELL-SHIELDED SECTION OF THE TRIPOD AND CONCENTRATED FIRE THERE WILL HAVE NO EFFECT.

The neighbours are getting suspicious of my 15-metre replica tripod

PLAN B

TANGLE LEGS

Don't be misled by the movies. Just tangling a rope between two trees won't be enough to bring down a real tripod, but a reinforced length of steel cable can do the job. It's important to keep the cable low until the last minute so that it doesn't show up on any tripod sensors. Ideally the cable should be raised and secured as the tripod first 'steps over', catching it mid-stride and snagging the rear leg. Tripod legs are retractable and the machine can balance on two legs for periods of time, so it's important that the tripod is moving forward when you ensnare the back leg.

PLAN C
HUMAN SUICIDE SCOOPER

One tactic that's particularly effective against the human scooper tripods is use of a Trojan Horse strategy. With this tactic one fighter allows himself to be lifted into the mesh basket and then reaches forward to ram a grenade or explosive into the nearest port. This is a risky operation and it's unlikely that either the attacker or those already in the basket will survive. It may be possible to replicate this form of attack on other models of tripod where ways can be found to get a fighter on top of a tripod to deliver the same explosive charge.

A COVERT TAKEOVER

This form of invasion is every conspiracy fan's worst nightmare. But, hey, just because you're paranoid, it doesn't mean you aren't right. The Draconians are a powerful alien species with whom we've had contact over thousands of years and we know these beings are sneaky – really sneaky. A covert takeover by any alien species such as the Draconians is to be both feared and guarded against. There won't be armies of saucers flying overhead or tripods stalking the planet. This will be <u>invasion by stealth,</u> with the gradual erosion of our free will and liberty until humanity wakes up one day and finds itself the servant of a new master!

▶ MOTIVATION

Uniquely among alien species, Draconians have an almost religious motivation to conquer and occupy a planet they often refer to as their home world. In Draconian folklore, there are even 'Earth Draconians' known as the Anunnaki who continue to exist within the Earth's core, sheltering patiently from the teeming mammals who now dominate the planet.

▶ CAPACITY TO WAGE WAR

After many years of war with the Insectoid species, <u>stealth is the Draconians' method of invasion.</u> They have a vast library of knowledge on humanity and potentially have clones in positions of influence on Earth already.

▶ STRATEGY AND TACTICS

Humanity won't see a Draconian invasion coming. These creatures work by stealth, cloaked and in the shadows. The Draconians are expert planners and manipulators. For the unprepared, the first sign that the reptilians have taken over will be when humans have to bow down to a new lizard boss at work!

▶ ALIEN RESILIENCE

With their longevity of life-span, the Draconians would think nothing of taking centuries to crush any human resistance on this planet. Draconians are careful planners and schemers and would easily adapt their plans in the face of any setback or misfortune. Thus the Draconian invasion timeline is over a very much longer period than with other scenarios. Indeed, many alien defence observers believe it's already in progress and we're on the countdown to contact.

SCENARIO DEBRIEF

The Draconian invasion is a patient one. These devious reptiles have a telling saying: 'The war that is won without fighting is the greatest victory.' But make no mistake – there'll be a century of hostile action before the Earth is finally renamed. Many of these attacks will be subtle. They'll have humans accusing other humans, persecuting innocent minorities and serving the invaders without even knowing it. By the time most of humanity wake up to the threat, it'll be far too late. Shape-shifting and clones will play their part, of course, but so will mass media, lies and deceit. And this secret invasion is for the long term.

Once in control, the Draconians may end up terra-forming Earth more to their liking. They may find a place for humanity serving in their palaces, bringing them their tasty mice snacks. But there again we may be seen as a costly and unnecessary hangover from another age in Earth's history.

DRACONIAN INVASION TIMELINE • SCENARIO 12132388/AA

CONTACT –100 YEARS

THE DRACONIANS DEVELOP A PLAN TO TAKE OVER THE EARTH

▶ Unlike other species, the Draconians don't regard their mission as an invasion – it's more akin to the liberation or retaking of a planet they view as one of their spiritual homes. Several plans have failed in the past few thousand years, but as a 'world culture' develops on Earth the Draconians judge that now is the time for them to take over. Previously they attempted to implant shape-shifted Draconians or cloned humans to rule empires on Earth.

CONTACT –20 YEARS

CLOAKED SHIP LANDINGS

▶ Draconian pod ships land around the world at strategic points. Draconians use any intelligence they have plus their shape-shifting ability to target key humans for cloning. A few shape-shifters work their way into positions of some influence.

CONTACT –15 YEARS

KIDNAPPINGS, DISAPPEARANCES AND THE REPTILIAN AGENDA

▶ With a network of targets identified, the Draconians work to replace key targets with cloned humans under their control. For the moment, they can manage the clones from their pod ships but this limits the number of clones to around 1,000. Key targets include young politicians, promising military officers and the brightest science students.

CONTACT –10 YEARS

THE CONSPIRACY

▶ The internet is awash with 'lunatics' talking about a Draconian takeover. They talk of shape-shifters and even clones, but most people have little interest. The real invaders help to spread rumours and misinformation.

▶ Meanwhile, first-generation clones have worked their way into positions of power as politicians, corporate heads, PR and marketing leaders, and senior members of the world's religions. The Draconians take a few calculated risks by manipulating several regional wars. This creates great levels of distrust between nations and keeps the general public preoccupied. Governments around the world tighten their civil laws against both real and imaginary threats.

▶ Part of the Draconian agenda is to create a malleable elite of uncloned humans to work with them, creating a small cadre or ruling class. Some are aware of the reptilian origin of their overlords, others aren't.

CONTACT

THE ALIENS ARRIVE

▶ The Draconians and their servants on Earth engineer a 'first contact' in which the reptilian race is finally revealed to the general populace. A few high-profile gifts of technology are given and mean that on the whole the invaders are welcomed. A pod-cruiser enters Earth's orbit, allowing the Draconians on Earth to harvest millions of clones.

CONTACT +10 DAYS

DRACONIAN LAW

▶ The final phase of the Draconians' agenda for control is gradually introduced. The continuing human leadership is progressively revealed to be incompetent. Some clones take a fall for their masters. Society is in danger of being destabilised by stealth. Law and order around the world is further tightened, including the introduction of Draconian law with, for example, public executions and trial without jury. It's made clear early on that Draconians aren't subject to Earth laws. The Draconians continue to appeal to humanity, presenting themselves as friends and guardians. They ensure that any abuses of power are associated with human rulers. Some of the populace start to think that they may be better off under the Draconians.

CONTACT +15 DAYS

THE NEW WORLD

▶ After years of chaos and economic stagnation, many call for the Draconians to take over power. Several move into positions of authority. They create incidents to discredit any uncontrolled human leaders of any ability. Soon Draconians and their clones are in every position of power.

CONTACT +20 DAYS

NEW DRACONIA

▶ Millions of Draconians arrive on Earth and start taking over. Soon humans are a rare sight in any large organisation or business. There are riots but these are put down by human police forces. The education level of humans collapses. The planet is renamed and grand plans for the establishment of huge stone temples are laid out. Some humans are invited to become citizens of New Draconia if they serve in Draconian military forces off-world.

STOPPING THE DRACONIANS

The Draconians are a reptilian species and it's important to understand some of the differences in how they think in order to do battle with them during their invasion of Earth. Firstly, with their extended life span of hundreds of Earth years, Draconians are remarkably patient by human standards. Secondly, they're covert in the extreme: if they feel that a curious human has uncovered part of their plan and that they cannot easily reach this individual to clone them, they'll often withdraw completely; many reports of Draconian plots come to nothing when they're investigated by the Ministry of Alien Defence. Thirdly, this species is highly adept at concealment and deceit, traits that have the unfortunate effect of making any human who tries to expose them appear 'delusional' when his or her claims are put under scrutiny.

ACTIONS HUMANITY CAN TAKE NOW

▶ The creation of a Draconian research institute to build on the important work already completed in China. Humanity must learn more about this elusive enemy.

▶ A comprehensive clone-spotting programme, including training for all police and security forces. Clones are an important weapon for the Draconians so action here is vital to prevent them infiltrating key positions.

▶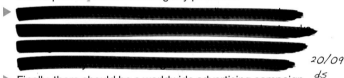

20/09
ds

▶ Finally, there should be a worldwide advertising campaign on how to spot a shape-shifter and a clone. Images of Draconians should be posted by officials so that everyone knows what to look out for.

▶ THE CLONING PROCEDURE

Life is precious to the Draconians. Well, to be more precise, reptilian life is precious to the Draconians and this species isn't known for taking risks. Even with their shape-shifting ability, it can be dangerous for a Draconian to move among an alien species.

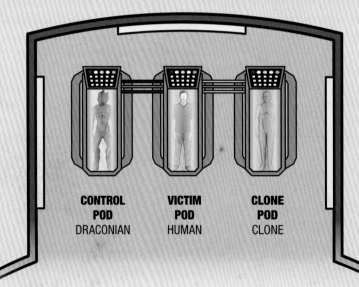

CONTROL POD
DRACONIAN

VICTIM POD
HUMAN

CLONE POD
CLONE

BEING ABLE TO SHAPE-SHIFT ENABLES DRACONIANS TO MOVE AMID HUMANITY WITHOUT AROUSING ANY SUSPICION. HOWEVER, IT WILL BE THE TARGETED USE OF CLONED HUMANS IN LARGE NUMBERS THAT WILL REALLY ENABLE THEM TO GET THEIR HANDS ON THE EARTH.

Ideally, Draconians require an original human being in order to create the best copies, but the process can also be completed with access to a significant DNA sample. We understand little of the science involved in the process, but we know that cloned humans are 'grown' over a period of hours in a clone pod. By using a cloned creation, the Draconians don't have to expose themselves to risk and only emerge for the most vital missions. Once a human duplicate has been created, the Draconian can take control at will; the original free-thinking human can return to regular life quite unaware that he or she has been cloned until the reptile takes control and disposes of them.

Check on Prince Charles – he has always been a supporter of reptile charities

CLOAKED OR CLONED?

A cloaked Draconian and a clone are two quite different things. Remember, being reptilian in origin, the Draconians have retained a chameleon-like ability to take on different forms. It's believed that they've enhanced this with bio-technology such that these aliens can now take on human form. Witnesses have reported that the 'cloaked' Draconians are excellent copies and can easily pass as humans.

However, the shape-shifting capabilities of the Draconians have their limitations. They can only stay in fully human form for around 24 hours; when they become tired they may increasingly flick between their original form and their human disguise. It's this phenomenon, known as 'shape-flicking', which people often catch sight of briefly. There are plenty of examples of shape-flicking photos on the internet but be warned that many are fake. Draconians are very cautious and ensure that they're in a secure location before they flick back into reptilian form.

Clones are copies of humans that have been 'reprogrammed' to serve their new alien masters. Technically speaking, clones aren't aliens as they're made with human DNA, but their loyalty is with their Draconian overlords. During the cloning procedure, it seems that Draconian instructions are hard-coded into the cloned human brain along with so-called slave knowledge acquired from the human host. When the Draconians invade, it's fully expected that they'll deploy tens of thousands of these clones.

HOW TO SPOT A CLONE

INEXACT COPIES

The process relies on DNA to reconstruct a human but there'll always be differences. If, for example, you knew a person before they were kidnapped and cloned, observe whether any skin blemishes have been removed – a scar or birthmark may have disappeared. Baldness is also something that cloning struggles to duplicate: if a balding senior business leader suddenly appears one day with a head of luscious hair, be very suspicious – this is a sure sign of cloning.

REDUCED LANGUAGE SKILLS

One drawback of transferring human data into a clone is that the clone can sometimes end up talking much more slowly than normal. It's often said that clones look like they're processing information with their vacant eyes when faced with an unusual word or a complex question – it may take a few seconds before they understand its meaning. This isn't due to any loss of intelligence on their part; it's because the Draconians are jamming far more information into the human brain and, as with any computer, the system runs more slowly.

SKIN DEGRADATION

One area where the Draconians really seem to struggle is in creating a clone that will last. No clone will last more than a year and they can appear to decline quite quickly as the months pass. As a rule, clones must check in with their reptilian overlords every three days, partly so this degradation process can be monitored. The main feature is dry skin, with redness. Clones need to use a great deal of moisturiser and tend to avoid extreme heat or cold.

SUSPECTED CLONES

The Draconians are focusing on cloning key individuals on Earth – people in positions of power and influence such as politicians, military leaders and world-famous entertainers. However, recent research has highlighted that more modest professions such as estate agents and traffic wardens are also high on the list of humans the Draconians wish to clone.

AN ALIEN WAR OF EXTERMINATION

We know from captured Grey intelligence that the Insectoid species controls vast swathes of other galaxies. Their hive shifts according to the whims of some commanding intelligence, possibly a Queen. However, their society is immensely sophisticated and structured. Typically there's no communication with the Insectoids by other species. Humanity is ill-equipped to counter a full-scale Insectoid invasion and our timeline provides worrying reading for military planners. The best chance for the survival of the human race would be an off-world strike on any hive ships as they enter our solar system, supported by a back-up plan for the evacuation of the planet.

▶ MOTIVATION

The Insectoids see all other life forms not just as inferior but as 'pollutants' and have been known to strip planets clean, leaving them sterile. If the Earth is in the path of one of their galactic migrations, they will seek to 'cleanse' it completely. They have no regard for any human achievement and will care nothing about destroying our planet.

▶ CAPACITY TO WAGE WAR

The Insectoids have a sophisticated war machine comprising hive ships and billions of armoured Insectoid soldier drones. We can expect some organic or biological weapons such as acidic spray, and Insectoids will adapt their drones according to the enemy they're facing.

▶ STRATEGY AND TACTICS

Hive ships arrive in our solar system and make their way towards orbit of either Earth or Mars. Humanity will then face a war with millions of soldier drones fired down to the planet's surface in landing pods. The only tactic the Insectoids use is to wipe out all human life.

▶ ALIEN RESILIENCE

This is a war of extermination and the Insectoids, with their massive numbers and single-minded ruthlessness, will carry on regardless of the casualties they suffer. All of our research suggests that there are billions and billions of Insectoids in the universe so it's going to be a very tough war for humanity.

SCENARIO DEBRIEF

It's estimated that humanity would last no more than eight weeks when facing an Insectoid invasion and this duration could be even shorter if two or more hive ships were to be dispatched. Indeed, every scenario run through the Ministry of Alien Defence military simulation computers ends the same way – with the complete extinction of human life on Earth.

In all scenarios Earth's military forces went head-to-head against the Insectoid horde and, after due reflection, military planning experts decided that we were simply fighting the 'wrong war'. In the scenarios we tried to 'outkill' the hive without fully understanding that even when the casualty figure for the Insectoids rose above one billion this still had no impact on their tactics or battle plans. From the moment a pod lands on a planet, the soldier drones are viewed as expendable.

It's clear that humanity needs to develop different strategies to deal with such a remorseless foe, but we would be very short of options. Debriefing concluded that the only real option would be a full evacuation of the planet.

INSECTOID INVASION TIMELINE • SCENARIO 12132100/EE

UNKNOWN

**AN EXPANSION
OF HIVE SPACE**

▶ A decision is made by the Insectoid race that our solar system is one of those now existing within their 'hive space'. From here on, any beings within the solar systems concerned are targets.

UNKNOWN

**A HIVE SHIP IS DESPATCHED
TO OUR SOLAR SYSTEM**

▶ The Insectoids send several ships into the various new segments of their 'hive space', including to our solar system. Distance is no obstacle: Insectoid space is millions of light years across and constantly being expanded. Drones may also be sent to ascertain whether any life forms exist within these regions.

**CONTACT
–1 MONTH**

**HIVE SHIP ENTERS
THE SOLAR SYSTEM**

▶ Hive ship enters our region of space, surveying planets and firing probes systematically as it closes towards the sun. If no life forms are discovered, a planet is declared 'cleansed'. The hive ship moves on a systematic course through our solar system.

CONTACT –10 DAYS

CONFUSION ON EARTH

▶ Scientists and other experts debate the nature of the mysterious object that has been discovered within our solar system. At first it's logged as an asteroid but its controlled trajectory soon ensures that it must be reclassified as a powered ship. However, some people remain confused owing to the fact that hive ships are hollowed-out asteroids.

CONTACT –5 DAYS

BOLTS FROM THE SKY

▶ Insectoid probes land on Earth for the first time. Several are destroyed. One identifies an evolved life form on the planet and transmits back to the hive ship. The hive ship is mobilised, millions of soldier drones are woken and millions more begin their hatching cycle.

CONTACT DAY

**THOUSANDS OF ROCK
PODS LAND OUTSIDE MAIN
POPULATION CENTRES**

▶ Rock pods fall to the ground in rural areas all over the world. When humans start to notice the phenomenon, some pods are destroyed by over-zealous local military forces. Each rock pod carries at least six soldier drones. The Insectoid invasion gathers pace as rock pods keep on landing and increasing numbers of soldier drones make their way towards large concentrations of humans, slaughtering anyone in their path.

CONTACT +3 DAYS

**LARGER WAVES OF PODS
LAND OUTSIDE MAIN
POPULATION CENTRES**

▶ Human forces fire everything in their arsenal at the emerging 'bugs'. The attacking soldier drones are hardy and well-armed, but can be destroyed. For a short while it appears that humanity may be getting the upper hand, despite immense casualties. Then a second, much larger wave begins to land. Their pattern ensures that this is a war without front lines. With soldier drones appearing in multiple locations, military organisation begins to strain.

CONTACT +7 DAYS

LOSS OF THE CITIES

▶ Every major city on Earth now belongs to the Insectoids and all we see are scenes of mass slaughter as the soldier drones work their way through key population centres. The remnants of any armed forces scatter into rural areas; some people head to colder regions where so far no Insectoids have been seen. Reports from the combat zones tell of a new, larger type of soldier drone that seems to be directing combat on the ground.

CONTACT +14 DAYS

THE WAR IS OVER

▶ Pockets of human resistance remain at both poles and in various mountain locations but all urban areas have been cleansed. Reports now tell of humans being gathered up for the first time and held prisoner by soldier drones.

CONTACT +30 DAYS

**PLANET EARTH
IS CLEANSED**

▶ Pods of specialist soldier drones land on Earth to wipe out what remains of human resistance. The billion or so soldier drones left on Earth retreat to caves and stay dormant. None of those sent down to Earth in pods is returned to the hive ship. The last remaining human prisoners are used as food until drones learn that their native fungus can grow in caverns on Earth. The soldier drones stay as a garrison, exterminating any remaining humans.

GUIDELINES FOR MILITARY FORCES

STOPPING THE INSECTOIDS

To the best of our knowledge, no civilisation at our level of technology has ever withstood an attack from the Insectoid species, with the possible exception of the Draconians. The UN computers ran over 1,000 simulations of Insectoid invasions where humanity went head-to-head with the invaders and in all but a handful the end result was human extinction. It's simply a game of numbers and humanity cannot possibly overcome the billions of drones sent once a hive engages with us. ▬▬▬▬▬▬▬▬▬▬▬▬ ▬▬▬▬▬▬▬▬▬▬▬▬ this means eradication, before the rest of the colony arrives. *14/06 ac*

HUMANITY'S ONLY HOPE

▶ Our only hope is to destroy a hive ship as soon as it's discovered. Once it gets close enough to Earth, it'll start to rain down landing pods of soldier drones, which are bio-engineered warriors designed to kill without fear. There should be no contact or declaration of war – an immediate attack must be undertaken. If delayed, drones will be launched but the destruction of the hive ship will at least stem the tide of drone attacks.

▶ Destruction of the hive ship in our system will buy humanity a crucial 'survival' window. More hive ships will eventually come but they may take years. Humanity shouldn't be complacent after this one defeat but use this crucial 'survival window of opportunity' to leave planet Earth forever and save mankind.

DESTRUCTION OF A HIVE SHIP

Any military analysis requires planners to look at the predicted invasion pattern of the enemy and then plan counter-moves to disrupt this action. Launching an attack into space will be the greatest technical challenge humanity has ever faced. We need to deliver an attack when the hive ship is approaching Earth as it's to be hoped that the Insectoids won't be expecting such an attack.

▶ **ASSEMBLE THE TEAM** A mix of combat engineers, drilling experts, special forces and civilian contractors – this is most likely to be a one-way trip.

▶ **EQUIP TWO SUPER SPACE SHUTTLES** The nations of the world will need to cooperate to get two super space shuttles into space and aim them for the hive ship.

▶ **DIVERSIONARY ATTACKS** If the super space shuttles are noticed by the Insectoids, a screen of other international ships will launch diversionary attacks.

▶ **LANDING ON THE HIVE SHIP** It's believed that hive ships don't have significant outer defences. The personnel will split into two teams. The drilling crew's task will be to dig into the rocky surface of the asteroid ship as far as possible and plant a nuclear device. The other crew will be a team of commandos sent to deliver further devices into the asteroid ship's propulsion system.

▶ **RETURN TO EARTH** Once the nuclear devices have been planted, some of the team will stay behind to ensure that they go off. The rest can clamber aboard one of the shuttles. Their chances of making it back to Earth are slim.

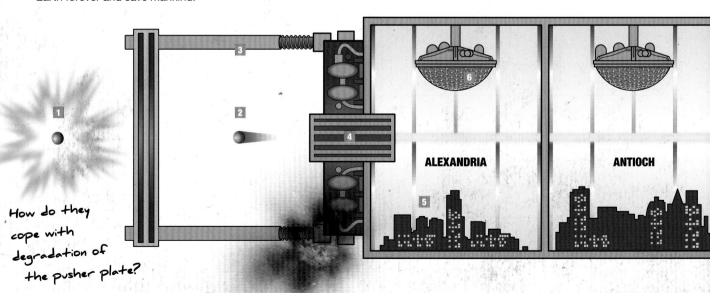

How do they cope with degradation of the pusher plate?

ALEXANDRIA

ANTIOCH

 MINISTRY OF ALIEN DEFENCE

OUR GREATEST CHALLENGE

Several alien invasion scenarios see humanity either forcibly evicted from Earth or threatened with such a sustained assault that extinction is probable. Part of the weakness of humanity is that we're restricted to Earth and its immediate orbit. We have no colonies within our own solar system, let alone further afield in other galaxies. In the case of the scenarios outlined above, our only chance to survive would be to leave Earth and in doing so face the greatest technical challenge ever presented to mankind.

We have discounted cryogenic technology as it's still in its infancy and have instead suggested a generational ship for some 300,000 survivors. For the curious we have issued answers to four FAQs:

▶ **How long would it take to build such a ship?**
Our estimate is 30–70 years.

▶ **Do we have the technology to build such a ship?**
Yes, the propulsion system and technology are available.

▶ **Seven billion people into a ship for 300,000? That doesn't add up.**
No, it doesn't. This ark ship is about saving humanity – we just don't have room for everyone.

▶ **Would the aliens let us leave in this ship? Wouldn't they just destroy it?**
This is a risk humanity must take.

FICTION IS FULL OF EXAMPLES OF INTERSTELLAR ARK SHIPS HEADING OUT INTO SPACE, THE LAST REFUGE OF A DYING SPECIES, DESIGNED TO WITHSTAND HUNDREDS, EVEN THOUSANDS, OF YEARS OF SPACE TRAVEL.

▶ THE GENERATION SHIP

1. The vast ship is propelled by a series of nuclear explosions – this process is known as 'nuclear pulse propulsion' and doesn't require the invention of any new technology. It measures 20 miles in length by 5 miles in diameter.

2. The ark ship has a supply of plutonium charges that are released every 1–10 seconds, allowing the ship to approach 0.7 light speed.

3. The ship's vast telescopic shock absorbers and pusher plate are two of the greatest engineering challenges of the project – they allow the vessel to withstand incredible forces as it accelerates into deep space.

4. The ark ship is equipped with supplementary thrusters and gigantic stores of spare parts and ore to enable many generations of ship's crew to conduct repairs to the hull over potentially hundreds or even thousands of years of inter-galactic space travel.

5. Four great cities have been built to house the remains of humanity – Alexandria, Antioch, Philadelphia and Tarsus. The cities are open to the interior of the ship, the sheer size of which leads to the emergence of a cool micro-climate that the inhabitants find congenial.

6. Agricultural bio-domes produce everything from food crops to industrial materials such as rubber. Each is sealed inside a reinforced dome and has a controlled climate.

7. A command station involves hundreds of crew members monitoring the vessel's key systems and is also equipped with various landing ships for use on arrival at New Earth.

8. The interior of the ark is lit by a central sun array that operates on a 24-hour cycle, creating a night and a day.

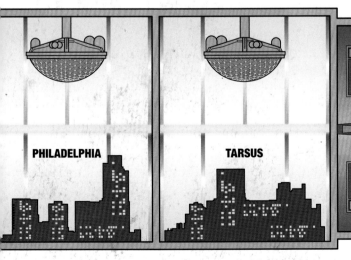

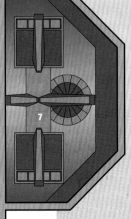

DEFENDING OUR PLANET

All military forces are designed with an enemy in mind and on Earth the enemies are mostly rival nations or political enemies. Our defence expenditure reflects this and the pace of our development of military technology is driven by this.

An alien invasion or covert action to take over the world represents a completely different threat from those our military forces are used to. Unless our forces adapt, they'll make little impact on extra-terrestrial invaders intent on enslaving humanity or taking over the planet. With this is mind, we've been granted permission to publish extracts from a security briefing made to the UN Security Council in 2010 by General Wilhelm Fokker, EU Defence Advisor to the UN. This is the first time any part of this briefing has been published.

THE PRINCIPLES OF MILITARY ACTION

Humanity faces a new threat – that of the alien invader – and our armed forces are ill-prepared. With the increasing scientific proof of life on other worlds and the evidence of alien intervention on our own planet, a major review of military policy and defence spending is essential.

Anyone who has studied the history of mankind can see what happens when a technologically advanced and ruthless invader attacks a culture that lacks the weapons and strategies to defend itself. The same principles will apply in any alien assault on Earth. We know that our opponent will be hundreds, maybe even thousands, of years ahead of us, using science and weaponry unknown to us. If we apply the military strategies and tactics we use against each other in our petty squabbles, there's no doubt that humanity will be annihilated.

But there's hope. Our studies have shown that with the right approach we can make a difference. We can blunt any alien incursion. With that in mind, I present a six-point plan that can be used by military forces around the world to plan, prepare and respond to an invasion from outer space.

> ALTHOUGH WE'RE FAR FROM A WORLD IN WHICH THE MILITARY FORCES OF PLANET EARTH CAN REALLY START TO WORK TOGETHER, IT'S THE RESPONSIBILITY OF THE MILITARY OFFICIALS OF EACH NATION TO CONSIDER THEIR DEFENCE PLANS AGAINST A THREAT FROM OUTER SPACE. I'M TALKING ABOUT AN INVASION BY EXTRA-TERRESTRIAL FORCES AS YET UNIDENTIFIED.
>
> **GENERAL WILHELM FOKKER, EU DEFENCE ADVISOR TO THE UN**

1 KNOW YOUR OPPONENT

Be clear on the type of species attacking the planet. Use the resources of the UN and organisations such as the Ministry of Alien Defence to identify the hostile alien regime. Ensure that the aliens have every opportunity to break off an attack.

2 INTELLIGENCE IS PARAMOUNT

Ignorance in military-response planning will finish off any organised human resistance. Make the capture of one alien aggressor a priority, particularly if it's a new species. Analyse for weaknesses, explore their technology. The chances are they'll know everything about us, but we'll know very little about them.

3 PROBING ATTACKS

Unless a real opportunity presents itself, avoid large-scale assaults on, for example, alien saucers or black triangle ships. Instead, use small, probing attacks. Look for gaps in their defences. Risk little until we know where their weaknesses lie and can coordinate an informed and effective attack.

4 FORCE ORGANISATION

Keep major military assets hidden until ready for use. Ensure that your military organisation is flexible, with few layers of command. Units must be able to operate independently as most alien attacks will focus on the infrastructure.

5 PREPARE FOR UNCONVENTIONAL WAR

The war against a full-scale alien invasion will be far from conventional so ensure that your forces have the capacity to adapt and deal with new tactics that may be unfamiliar to conventional military planners.

6 LEARN, ADAPT AND LEARN AGAIN

There are so many unknowns involved in planning for an invasion from space that sometimes effective military preparation is almost impossible. Ensure that you have a robust organisation that can cope with a massive strike at the centre.

KNOW YOUR ENEMY!

Being able to spot a hostile object in the sky and knowing the difference between one of our own advanced fighters and an attacking extra-terrestrial ship is a vital skill for everyone. Use this chart to help test yourself – how well do you know these profiles? Are you still confusing Grey saucers with Draconian pod ships? Study hard and ensure that you know the difference.

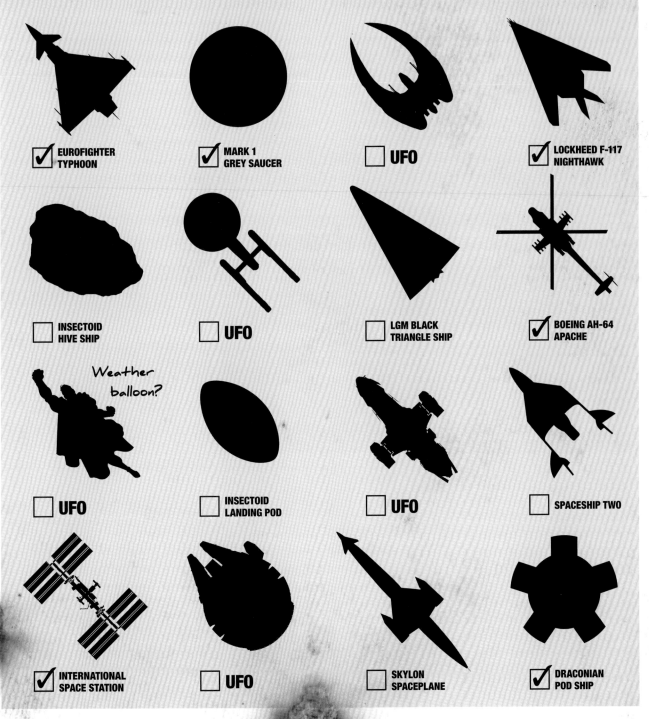

☑ EUROFIGHTER TYPHOON

☑ MARK 1 GREY SAUCER

☐ UFO

☑ LOCKHEED F-117 NIGHTHAWK

☐ INSECTOID HIVE SHIP

☐ UFO

☐ LGM BLACK TRIANGLE SHIP

☑ BOEING AH-64 APACHE

Weather balloon?

☐ UFO

☐ INSECTOID LANDING POD

☐ UFO

☐ SPACESHIP TWO

☑ INTERNATIONAL SPACE STATION

☐ UFO

☐ SKYLON SPACEPLANE

☑ DRACONIAN POD SHIP

DEFENDING OUR PLANET

DEFENCE IN SPACE

If humanity is serious about surviving in a universe teeming with alien life forms, then the defence of our home world must start in space. Ideally, we should be in a position to declare a 'Monroe Doctrine' for our solar system, including the Sun, Earth, the rest of the inner planets and the outer planets as well as all moons, comets and meteoroids therein. The outer mark would

THE WORLD'S TOP 15 COUNTRIES IN TERMS OF MILITARY INVESTMENT SPEND OVER $1,700 BILLION ANNUALLY ON FORCES THAT WE NOW KNOW WOULD BE LARGELY USELESS AGAINST ALIEN INVADERS. IMAGINE IF WE SPENT JUST HALF OF THAT TO FUND THE CREATION OF AN EARTH DEFENCE FORCE, WHICH WOULD HAVE A BRIEF TO OPERATE BEYOND THE EARTH'S ATMOSPHERE.

be Pluto but with a monitoring zone far beyond, including the Kuiper Belt Objects. The defence of humanity must be seen in a bigger perspective than just the defence of Earth.

Fast-forward a few decades and we'll require massive advances in virtually every area of science if we're to start truly safeguarding our planet from alien invasion. A viable space propulsion system, the development of effective space fighters, the creation of working energy shields, advances in space architecture with which to build long-term space stations and on-world structures – the list can seem both endless and daunting. But we're making progress and if we combine the brains, ingenuity and resources of humanity for this crucial project we may just stand a chance.

▶ OUTER SOLAR SYSTEM

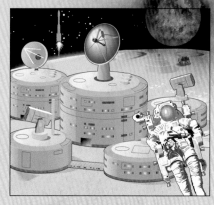

PLUTO
LISTENING STATIONS

Listening stations on Pluto will be our first line of defence until humanity has developed deep-space cruisers. We should seek constantly to be pushing these stations further out into space, creating a buffer zone in which we can detect any ship movements. The challenge would be to pick up ships in hyperspace but we have so little understanding of the science involved in detecting them.

KUIPER BELT
SPACE MINE FIELDS

Prudent use of space mines to cover some of the more exposed approaches may be vital to restrict ship movements. This is a controversial recommendation: unless 'intelligent' mines are created, we could end up destroying both friend and foe. With our current level of technology space mines would at best merely slow down an enemy, and it must be remembered that most alien ships are equipped with energy shielding.

TRITON
DEFENSIVE OUTPOST

A defensive outpost on the largest of Neptune's moons would be home to a specially trained first-contact squadron of space fighters. Triton is an ideal location for an off-world base to accommodate our first interception force. It's unlikely that our star fighters would last long in ship-to-ship warfare with an advanced alien species so the primary objective would be to get fighting forces on board enemy ships, to disrupt, delay and destroy.

DEFENDING OUR PLANET
CREATING A FASTER-THAN-LIGHT DRIVE

$$J = \pi\rho\int_0^R\left(R^2-z^2\right)^{\frac{3}{2}}dz = A = \oint\vec{F}\,d\vec{l} = 0$$
$$= \pi\rho\left[\int_0^R R^3\,dz - 2\int_0^R R^2 x^2\,dz\right] + \int_0^{\ell} x^3 a\int\frac{dx}{\cos x}$$
$$e^2 = mF^2$$

If you really want to do your bit for humanity and have a keen interest in science, you could do a great service for your planet by developing a propulsion system that can move objects faster than the speed of light – in effect to create warp capability. Sneakily, we've hidden two challenges in there:

▶ To provide either mathematical or experimental proof that we can make an object move faster than light.
▶ Mount this new propulsion system on a space vehicle.

It may be worth reading up a bit about the background to the challenge. Power generation and manipulation will be crucial so don't attempt any experiments if you're on a 'pay as you go' electricity meter as you may require the energy of a small sun to move an object at light speed.

▶ **299,792,458 METRES PER SECOND**

This is the speed of light and with this figure in mind you should be ready to start work. Remember – always check your maths. Please send any proof of success to the Ministry of Alien Defence in London.

KEEPING OUR PLANET SAFE FROM ALIEN INVADERS IS GOING TO TAKE THE COMBINED RESOURCES OF HUMANITY. SO, IF YOU DON'T THINK OF YOURSELF AS 'SCIENCEY' THEN REMEMBER THERE ARE PLENTY OF CHALLENGES STILL OUT THERE, FROM HUNTING DOWN SHAPE-SHIFTING LIZARDS ON EARTH TO WATCHING OUT FOR CLONES IN POSITIONS OF POWER. PLUS, ANY EARTH DEFENCE FORCE WILL ALWAYS NEED GOOD PEOPLE TO MAN THAT LISTENING POST ON PLUTO.

▶ INNER SOLAR SYSTEM

MARS
MILITARY BASE

There would be a substantial military base of operations on the North Pole of Mars, forming the home port of the Earth Defence Fleet. Responsible for outer system patrols and deep-space missions, it would be supported by a permanent station in orbit. With several thousand people, this site would serve as a 'species reserve' so that humanity isn't completely wiped out in the event of Earth being destroyed .

VENUS
COVERT BASE

The role of this site would be the preparation and maintenance of humanity's big escape plan – the ark ships – by a team of scientists and engineers. A fully prepared ark ship would be ready at a few days' notice to head off into deep space should Earth be threatened. Pre-selected people would be evacuated to the base and, from there, fired into deep space with an Earth-like planet as their target.

EARTH
ARMED SATELLITES

A ring of armed satellites would hamper any attempted landing on Earth and provide a planetary force field, supported by a set of ground-based planetary batteries that could fire high into the Earth's orbit. Once we have the technologies required to create these weapons, they could be deployed to protect any planetary body where humanity may settle in its 'post-Earth' existence.

DEFENDING OUR PLANET

► SPACE MARINE CORPS

The men of the Space Marine Corps would be known as Heinlein troopers, after the great science-fiction writer who foresaw that we would still need 'soldiers' to fight in space and hostile conditions, equipped with amazing new technologies.

1 A cadet would have to complete the toughest military training on Earth before being able to join the Space Marine Corps for a minimum of five years' service.

2 Space marines typically fight in pressurised armour suits that are linked directly to the soldier's brain, allowing instant and instinctive control.

3 The powered armour suit allows the marine to fight in all conditions as well as giving him enhanced strength and instant access to an array of weapons.

4 Powered armour suits also allow marines to travel short distances by utilising mini-jets.

► The space suits of today's astronauts are poorly suited to any form of combat. The development of a Space Marine Corps complete with the right weapons, combat attire and equipment would be a lynchpin in any defence of humanity.

► SPACE FIGHTER

The space shuttle programme under NASA made huge advances in the use of reusable vehicles and brought us closer to the dream of a fully equipped, combat-ready space fighter. The Russian, Chinese and Indian space programmes would be integral to the creation of the first space fighter.

1 A crew of three would pilot this advanced space fighter; they would be selected as elite pilots from a Space Flight Training Academy, made up of the world's best pilots from every nation. In space, the only insignia would be the 'The Corps'.

2 A bio-computer based on captured Grey technology would allow the ship's multiple systems and weapons to be controlled via the pilot's neuro-interface.

3 The propulsion system would be designed using other alien technology, and the hybrid weapons would include ship-destroying missiles as well as the world's most powerful lasers; these would fire for only 30 seconds due to their power requirements.

4 The space fighter, which could travel at close to light speed for a short time, would be designed primarily for combat within our solar system, operating from a base ship.

Once we start to make effective use of the alien technology we've acquired, we won't be far from having the capability to develop a working prototype of a real space fighter. The real challenge will be the propulsion technology and weaponry.

Where do I sign up for this? I've seen Independence Day and every Starship Troopers movie – I'm ready to rock!

SPACE BATTLE CRUISER

With Earth forces operating throughout the solar system and beyond, our fleets will need at least one class of capital ship to provide heavy weapons and support. With the incredible cost required to build such ships, it would be logical to opt for a single class of 'battle cruiser' which, as in naval history, delicately balances armour, speed and firepower.

1 This Asimov-class battle cruiser would be powered by a captured anti-matter drive from a crashed LGM triangle ship. Although tiny, this drive could be reverse-engineered into the ship and provide propulsion and pulse cannons to defend the vessel.

2 The ship would also be equipped with a larger and more powerful version of the space fighter laser, which is designed for ship-to-ship combat.

3 The anti-matter drive would provide power for rudimentary shield technology, which would surround the ship but offer a relatively weak field of protection.

4 The Asimov-class ship would carry a complement of over 2,000 space marines together with a squadron of nine space fighters.

In reality, the technical challenges in designing and building an Asimov-class battle cruiser are immense. For example, we currently only have three LGM anti-matter drives on Earth and with our limited knowledge it could be disastrous to try to place one of these units in an Earth ship. Nevertheless, to properly defend our solar system, we'll need these robust and hard-working ships.

SPACE INFRASTRUCTURE

To operate effectively far beyond Earth, humanity will require space stations in orbit as well as planet-based facilities. Even with the benefit of an advanced propulsion system, our fleet will need base ships throughout the solar system to service and support them. Space architecture covers the engineering expertise and knowledge we need to build both orbiting space stations and bases on other planets.

1 This Hawking-class space station would orbit Mars and provide berthing for a single battle cruiser at a time as well as multiple shuttles and fighters.

2 The crew of 1,000 would mainly comprise maintenance workers, servicing everything from fighters to listening posts.

3 The station could defend itself with pulse cannon but its gravity generator would use most of its power.

4 Hawking-class space stations would be designed to have families on board – if the Earth is destroyed, these communities will become outposts of humanity.

The benefit of the Hawking-class space station is its ability to be dragged into position and even moved if required. It uses it own propulsion systems just to maintain orbit. Fixed surface bases would doubtless be more secure but Earth may start with mobile stations before investing in surface facilities. It's likely that construction would develop from the current International Space Station before human forces reach out further into our solar system with bases on Mars and Venus.

ALIEN INVASION EXAM

ALIEN DEFENCE
BASIC LEVEL

Remember G.L.D.I. –
Grey, Little Green Men,
Draconian, Insectoid!

You now have the chance to test your alien defence knowledge and skills and achieve a nationally recognised qualification. Achieving a Basic Certificate in Alien Defence is something you can add to your CV and will show potential employers that you take the alien threat seriously.

INSTRUCTIONS TO CANDIDATE

▶ You should attempt all questions on the paper.
▶ You must base your answers on the content of this manual.
▶ No sneaky cheating.
▶ For the 20 questions, you should score 15 or above to pass.
▶ This is a closed-book examination lasting 45 minutes.

1 Which of the following describes how you feel about the alien threat to Earth?

A Alien defence is for nutcases and lunatics.

B This manual has opened my eyes to the threats out there in space.

C Yeah, maybe they're out there but I'm not convinced. Greys, Little Green Men – all sounds a bit X-files to me.

D There are no such things as aliens.

2 What does the United Nations Organisation for Earth Defence do?

A Not much by the sounds of it.

B Is it causing global warming?

C It's an organisation that coordinates alien defence work around the world.

D They're the people who make sure that all of Europe's bananas are straight.

3 What is the Extra-Terrestrial Security Act of 1979.

A It's government legislation that enshrines in law the principles of defence against aliens.

B It enables aliens to work among us.

C They want to ban the movie about ET.

D Nothing – because it's all made-up rubbish.

4 Which of the following is not a motivation classification according to the UNED alien invasion matrix?

A Scavengers – they come to loot our planet and humanity for resources they can use.

B Exterminators – they want to eradicate humanity. Not good!

C Spice-meisters – the aliens have come to Earth in search of ever hotter spices.

D Observers – neutral aliens who seek only to watch humanity and events on Earth.

5 You notice a reptilian face in a reflection – what do you do?

A Nothing, I like people who have a little bit of the lizard about them – it can be very sexy.

B Think little of it – I see lots of strange things.

C Discretely turn and follow the individual and find her ship – she's clearly a Draconian.

D Pretend I didn't see anything.

6 You meet a glowing Nordic alien. She asks you about Earth. What do you say?

A Tell her it's a cool place with loads of fighting and that she's pretty tough herself.

B Go into detail on how many amazing species have disappeared from the planet and that it's not as good as it used to be.

C Talk about great human achievements.

D Talk about your favourite reality TV show.

7 What caused the Grey saucer to crash at Roswell in 1947?

A Nothing. Officially it was a weather balloon.

B Agent Mulder told me it was the Smokin' Man. Hang on, or was it Agent Skinner?

C The UFO was shot down by a jet fighter – yeah, they got what was coming to them.

D The saucer crash is most likely to have been caused by a young alien drunk on 'gleek'.

8 What is an ET prepper?

A Hardcore fans of the Steven Spielberg film who re-enact whole scenes of his movie.

B Someone obsessed with science fiction.

C A paranoid nutcase with an obsession about tin-foil and too much time on their hands.

D Someone who has learned about the alien threat and is doing something about it.

9 What is an anti-mind-probe hat and what is it made of?

A It's one part paranoia, one part crazy and it's made of good old insanity.

B I don't know. Was that even in the manual?

C It's a resistance tool that can be worn to protect from alien mind probing

D I'm wearing one now – I like to wear it at a jaunty angle as I look like a gangster.

10 You spot a mutilated cow in the corner of a field. What do you do?

A Seek out the farmer and hand him a leaflet on Greys and cattle mutilation.

B Write a strongly worded letter to the council.

C Go home and join the World Wildlife Fund – someone has to protect these animals.

D Go back to the car and head to the nearest steak house.

11 You awake in the night to find light streaming through the window. What do you do next?

A Dash for my alien safe room.

B Turn over and go back to sleep.

C Hide under the bed – they might fly away.

D Party like it's 1999.

12 You see a dark triangle-shaped ship flying through the air. What do you think to yourself?

A That is a black triangle ship. I must report this sighting immediately.

B Look at it, think how much you like triangles, then go for a pizza.

C I don't see anything, aliens don't exist. I think I'm a clone.

D I wonder what time dinner is?

MINISTRY OF ALIEN DEFENCE

13 **You wake up in a cold metal room. What do you do next?**

A Look for the phone and call room service.

B Wait for the cleaner to arrive.

C Wait for the aliens to return to see if you can talk them into returning you.

D Survey the room. You've been abducted and you need to find a way out fast.

14 **Silver saucers appear over every major city in the world. What's happening?**

A The great ones are here. I would go home and create a large placard welcoming them.

B This is an invasion of the species known as the Insectoids. I would arrogantly share this knowledge with all who would listen.

C Clearly the Greys. My analysis is that this is the precursor to a full-scale invasion.

D I'd use this as a chance to snap up a few cheap properties.

15 **Which of the following is the favoured weapon of a Little Green Man?**

A A hand-held body probing weapon.

B A trans-dimensional warp coil.

C Razor-sharp wit.

D A small classic-type alien ray gun.

16 **An asteroid ship is on a course for Earth. The ship starts firing cylinders towards Earth. What is your assessment?**

A This is surely good news as we may become close friends with these new aliens.

B Bad news. Insectoids use this type of ship. We need to prepare for a world of pain.

C It'll be like having another moon.

D If we remain quiet, they might just go away.

17 **Which of the following best describes the Little Green Men?**

A Trustworthy space scientists.

B Hippies of the universe spreading love.

C Nasty, spiteful creatures.

D Martians who envy Earth and are keen heavy-metal fans.

18 **How can you best spot a Draconian clone?**

A Ask honestly, 'Are you a clone?'

B If the individual laughs uncontrollably at your jokes it's surely a clone.

C I don't believe in clones.

D It may have stunted speech, lack a belly button and its skin may be dried out.

19 **Which of the following changes can substantially reduce your chances of being abducted by aliens?**

A Move to a nice house in the country where they can't find me.

B Layers of foil in the ceiling, wooden locks on the doors and a fully kitted out anti-abduction room.

C Work for NASA, trying to contact the aliens and convincing them we mean no harm.

D Join an alien-worshipping cult – they will never take one of their own followers.

20 **Which of the following phrases best describes an Insectoid invasion?**

A It should be a walk in the park for humanity. There won't be any major problems with defeating the bugs – we could just use a bit of insect repellent.

B Insectoids would never invade – they're far too polite.

C Bugs, what bugs? Run... everyone run... we're all going to die!

D An Insectoid invasion would be a major challenge to humanity – they would come in great numbers and Earth is unlikely to survive as we know it.

ANSWERS

20 D	19 B
18 D	17 C
16 B	15 D
14 C	13 D
12 A	11 A
10 A	9 C
8 D	7 D
6 C	5 C
4 C	3 C
2 C	1 B

YOUR SCORE • BASIC LEVEL

15–20 You achieved the required standard and are awarded a Certificate of Competency in Alien Defence. You have clearly learned from the lessons and expertise within this manual. Well done – humanity needs people like you. But, don't stop there. Keep learning and developing your skills to face an alien invasion.

10–14 You have obviously learned a lot from this manual but there are gaps in your knowledge. Try to look back through the sections and identify these knowledge gaps. You've made a good start but you still have a lot of work to do.

0–9 This is a very poor result. Did you just pick up this book and flick right to the back? Reread all of the chapters and you may want to take in some good science-fiction movies. You still seem to doubt the threat of an alien invasion. Maybe you won't be convinced until a Little Green Man pops up and vaporises you.

In 2014 the Ministry of Alien Defence launched a series of educational qualifications aimed at developing public awareness in areas such as abduction prevention and alien invasion awareness. The idea was to provide a basic level of education to everyone in the country. The result was the Certificate of Competency in Alien Defence, which is the equivalent of an NVQ Level 3.

The alien defence certification programme will be rolled out over the next few years. It is hoped that greater levels of education among the public will create a better environment for a real debate on Earth's preparedness for an invasion from space. We did try to get this included in the core curriculum in schools in England and Wales but the government insisted that maths and English had to stay.

ALIEN INVASION EXAM

ALIEN DEFENCE
ADVANCED LEVEL

Me? On the edge?
Tell me something new...

Do not attempt the Advanced Level paper until you have completed your basic defence qualification. The Advanced Level Certification provides you with a survival profile that can be assessed after you have completed the survey questions. Answer honestly.

1 The Haynes Alien Invasion Manual is:

A Quite a funny book that I also use as a tray for my TV dinners.

B Ha ha ha – I like aliens and stuff like that.

C I'm now embarking on a programme to abduction-proof my home.

D This is it man. This is hardcore. This manual is going save humanity man.

2 What is the speed of light?

A It's how quickly I get out of work on a Friday.

B Give Professor Stephen Hawking a call.

C It's a universal constant that's important in many areas of physics.

D It's what we need to ensure that the alien scum can never threaten our planet again.

3 Which of the following phrases best describes your understanding of the Treaty of Greada signed in 1955?

A Treaty of what? Mmmm, I'm not sure – was it something to do with breakfast cereal?

B Was it that we were allowed to go on a trip in one of their flying saucers?

C This was the first formal agreement between humanity and an alien species.

D It was a mistake. Never deal with aliens.

4 Who are the Men in Black?

A Galaxy defenders who make movies.

B I don't know but they sound sinister.

C They're the thin line that defends humanity against hostile alien acts.

D They defend people against aliens but in my view they should do more.

5 What does ET prepping mean to you?

A OK, I know this one. Is it reading this book?

B It's about aliens and maybe sticking up some tin-foil here and there.

C It's a way of life. It's about being educated and trained to resist alien intervention.

D It means sitting in a darkened room staring at pictures of aliens for 12 hours a day.

6 Giant saucers appear over the cities of Earth. What's your reaction?

A Keep on watching Jerry Springer reruns.

B Go outside and watch the dancing lights.

C Rush back home and grab my alien invasion bag – things are about to get frosty.

D Grab the weapon I keep by my side at all times and get ready to 'take out the trash'.

7 We know of four alien species who have plans to invade Earth. What's your reaction to this statement?

A I loved ET – it was my favourite film.

B If there are aliens then why aren't they here now? This is nonsense. Pure nonsense.

C I wasn't convinced before, but after reading this manual I've changed my mind.

D Good. I'm glad they're coming here.

8 You find yourself in a sterile white cell. What do you do?

A Close my eyes and try to wake up.

B Conclude that I'm stuck in a bad hospital. I should have paid for better healthcare.

C Weigh up my options and formulate an escape plan. This is an alien abduction.

D It's an alien abduction and think to myself, 'This is it, man, this is it!".

9 A friend tells you she's had a close encounter. What's your reaction?

A Insist that she sees a psychiatrist.

B Make beeping noises every time she speaks.

C Tell her to write everything down and report it to the Ministry of Alien Defence.

D Wrestle her to the floor, checking to see if she's a clone or has any implants.

10 Which of the following would be your catch phrase for an alien invasion?

A 'If I close my eyes, they go away.'

B 'Aliens! We're all going to die!!!'

C 'Stay quiet, keep watching and wait for the right time to strike.'

D 'Hey ET, I was born to die but I'm sure gonna take a few of you with me!'

11 You come across a bunker, all supplied and ready to go. What do you do?

A I don't like small spaces so leave it.

B Make a note to tell the owners that they should always lock their secret bunkers.

C Check it out – it may be useful.

D Forget hiding – have a quick look to see if there are any cool weapons down there.

12 An alien tripod appears above a lorry full of refugees. It's about to open fire with its ray gun. What do you do?

A Put my fingers in my ears and start humming my favourite Abba song.

B Remind myself to stay off the roads.

C Use my alien defence knowledge to try to distract the tripod away from the survivors.

D Run towards the alien tripod swinging a baseball bat and screaming.

13 The invasion is over and humanity has been crushed under the small boot of the Little Green Men. The commander offers you the chance to join the LGM human forces. How do you respond?

A Laugh and tweak his cute little nose.

B Ask if you can phone a friend.

C Accept his offer, knowing that certain vaporisation awaits you if you refuse.

D Reach for his ray gun, grab it and start vaporising every green man in a suicidal shooting spree around the alien complex.

14 You spot a Draconian dragging a celebrity into a black car. It's a kidnapping. What's your reaction?

A I'd walk on by. They don't exist.

B I'd watch them for a bit – it's not something you see every day.

C I'd hail a cab and discretely follow them.

D Aliens! Here on Earth! I would run towards the Draconian.

15 You suspect that you may be a clone. What do you do next?

A I don't believe in all this clone nonsense. I'd keep on living the dream like normal.

B I'd go with it and see where it leads.

C I'd complete a medical check of myself. Do I have a belly button?

D I would turn myself into the authorities.

16 You come across a crashed saucer. Greys are lying around but the saucer is in good shape. What do you do next?

A I would help them back into their ship.

B I would run. I might tell someone later on.

C I would make sure the injured Greys stay alive as they could be useful.

D I would open up a whole world of pain on the Greys then take their ship.

17 The Draconians have taken over and Earth is within their control. A Nordic shimmers into view. What do you say?

A You ask him how he gets his platinum blond hair so shiny and full of body.

B Nordics are powerful aliens: you ask him to kill all the Draconians and clones.

C You plead with him for help.

D You tell him that now's the time to put up or shut up. No more talkie-talkie.

18 The government issues a request for volunteers to intercept an Insectoid hive ship. How do you respond?

A Continue playing on the X-Box.

B Distribute leaflets – someone might be interested.

C Weigh up my skills and decide I'd be better used battling the aliens on Earth.

D Sign up – if there's going to be alien killing then I want in.

19 We need an Earth Defence Force because?

A It would be just like in *Star Trek* and we could all get to wear cool jump suits.

B I'm not sure we need it. It would cost a lot and there's plenty to be done around here.

C If we channel our defence spending into such a force we could develop the capability to defend our planet.

D It's the best chance a loose cannon like me has of getting into space.

20 What should the priorities be for humanity in terms of new inventions?

A I'd like a Furbie that keeps on working for years and years.

B We should invent the flying car then focus on the challenges of global warming.

C Humanity should focus all resources on developing a space propulsion system.

D We need super star fighters with enough firepower to destroy a planet.

The Advanced Level alien defence certification is designed to discover your 'prepping profile'. Extensive work by psychologists has revealed that there are only four types of ET preppers and you need to fall into one of the last three categories to achieve your advanced certification. The Advanced Certificate of Competency in Alien Defence is a classification that you should use to develop your skills and profile within the ET prepping community.

YOUR SCORE • ADVANCED LEVEL

Is 'planning to kick ET's butt' a profile?

▶ **MOSTLY As**

You have a ray gun target on your back. You have been watching too much reality TV and none of the wisdom in this manual seems to have sunk in. Please reread the entire book, taking notes as you go along.

'MOST LIKELY TO BE ABDUCTED, LEAST LIKELY TO KNOW WHAT'S GOING ON. WILL BE OF NO HELP IN SAVING HUMANITY.'

▶ **MOSTLY Bs**

Your chances of making it through an alien invasion are slim. You lack alien defence knowledge and should carefully reread this manual. You need to be clear that aliens exist and take the threat more seriously.

'THERE IS POTENTIAL HERE BUT A LOT OF WORK TO BE DONE. THESE INDIVIDUALS NEED TO MAKE ALIEN DEFENCE A PRIORITY.'

▶ **MOSTLY Cs**

You are a well-balanced human ready to defend your planet. You have the knowledge you will need to survive but you need to work hard to become a real ET prepper. Consider dedicating more time to your alien-monitoring activities.

'THESE PEOPLE ARE THE FRONT LINE IN OUR DEFENCE AGAINST THE ALIENS. THEY ARE PREPARED FOR ANY INVASION.'

▶ **MOSTLY Ds**

You are a human on the edge. Some may find your 'in the face' style uncomfortable but humanity needs 'gung-ho, ask questions later' lunatics like you. Don't ever change. Just make sure you use your energy wisely.

'ISOLATED LONERS, WITH A HINT OF CRAZY ABOUT THEM, THESE INDIVIDUALS COULD SAVE OR DOOM HUMANITY.'

Certificate in Alien Defence

This is to certify that

_____

has successfully completed all prescribed

requirements and is hereby designated a

Basic Level Alien Invasion Survivor

In testimony whereof, we have subscribed our signature

under the seal of the Ministry of Alien Defence

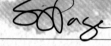

_____   _____
Ministry of Alien Defence   Signature Witness

Certificate in Alien Defence

This is to certify that

_____

has successfully completed all prescribed

requirements and is hereby designated an

Advanced Level Alien Invasion Survivor

In testimony whereof, we have subscribed our signature

under the seal of the Ministry of Alien Defence

_____   _____
Ministry of Alien Defence   Signature Witness